How To

A Day ... Life,
Or the Answer to the Question,
How Can I Live A Holy Life?

Metropolitan Gregory (Postnikov)
1784-1860 of St. Petersburg

Original Russian printed in 1904

Seraphim F. Englehardt, translator
*Translated from the 1994 Russian
edition by the publisher, "Otchii Dom"*

Holy Trinity Publications
The Printshop of St Job of Pochaev
Holy Trinity Monastery
Jordanville, New York
2012

Printed with the blessing of His Eminence,
Metropolitan Hilarion First Hierarch
of the Russian Orthodox Church Outside of Russia

How To Live A Holy Life
© 2005 Holy Trinity Monastery

Sixth Printing: Holy Trinity Publications, 2023

PRINTSHOP OF
SAINT JOB OF POCHAEV

An imprint of

HOLY TRINITY PUBLICATIONS
Holy Trinity Monastery
Jordanville, New York 13361-0036
www.holytrinitypublications.com

ISBN: 978-0-88465-089-8 (Paperback)
ISBN: 978-0-88465-366-0 (ePub)
ISBN: 978-0-88465-367-7 (Mobi/Kindle)

TABLE OF CONTENTS

APPEAL TO THE CHRISTIAN

Do you call yourself a Christian? Are you a Christian in actual fact? Do you live as a Christian should live, that is, do you fervently desire and earnestly seek after that which a true Christian desires and seeks after? The blessings that the Lord promises the true Christian in the future life are to be highly desired. And inexpressibly horrible is the misfortune into which sin plunges us, if we do not desire and do not seek what a Christian must desire most fervently and seek after most earnestly. What will happen if you do not receive the promised blessings and are cast into eternal torments? You have already lived a considerable time, but have you ever asked yourself these and similar questions? In particular, have you ever contemplated upon them seriously?

The Christian must be such as was Jesus Christ. *Let this mind be in you, which was also in Christ Jesus*, said the holy Apostle Paul (Phil. 2:5). Are you the kind of person that Jesus Christ was? Do you behave as He did? Do you live by His teaching, or Gospel, that He gave us as a rule of life?

A Christian must not love the world (I John 2:15). But many are completely bound to the world, so that it seems like they live only for the world: they always think like the world, they behave like the world, and all the rules that they follow in their likes are precisely those rules that the world follows. Aren't you such a person? Such a life is not a Christian one and is quite disastrous.

The Lord once said in the Old Testament through the holy prophet to His Chosen People: *Judge, I pray you, betwixt me and my vineyard. What could have been done more to my vineyard, that I have not done in it? wherefore, when I looked that it should bring forth grapes, brought it forth wild grapes? And now go to; I will tell you what I will do to my vineyard: I will take away the hedge thereof, and it shall be eaten up; and break down the wall thereof, and it shall be trodden down* (Isa. 5:3-5). Can not the Lord God with incomparably greater right in the New Testament tell us who are disobedient to Him, "What could I do for you that I have not done? I redeemed you with My Blood, gave birth to you in the bosom of My church; enlightened you with the light of the true faith, gave you all the means and abilities for salvation, prepared eternal blessedness for you and constantly in every way disposed you to seek this blessedness. Did I not sufficiently show My love for you? Wretches! I became your Savior and try in every way to lead all of you into eternal blessedness, but you only endeavor in every way not to find yourself in eternal blessedness, but for Me to become your judge and give you up to eternal torments. I created you to be eternally with Me and to experience My joys, but you behave yourselves in such a way that I would abhor you and repudiate you. I am very merciful towards you, but you by your ingratitude and your self-will try only to enflame My anger toward you. Neither My mercy, which I constantly show you, nor eternal blessedness, to which I so often and so earnestly call you, nor the terrible torments of hell, with which I threaten you, rouse you onto the path of salvation. Would it not have been better for you if you had not been born and the light of faith had not shone on you?" My friend, what if one day we shall have to hear such words from the Lord? Such words even now, when we have not yet heard them, tear at the heartstrings. What will it be like when we do hear them and when we have to reap what we have sown for ourselves by our sins? Have fear in your heart!

Cease your customary way of life and begin to live according to the Lord's teaching, which is written in His Holy Gospel, a God-pleasing, holy life.

So that you will be able to more quickly get started, I offer instructions for one day. If you faithfully follow these instructions, you will see that you will need no other instructions. You should pass every subsequent day just as you did the first one.

HOW SHOULD WE CONDUCT OURSELVES IN THE MORNING?

In the morning, conduct yourself in the following manner:

1. Upon awakening, try first of all to direct your thoughts to the Lord God. Directing our thoughts to the Lord God should be our most natural activity at every other time of the day as well, because there is absolutely no one who could be so necessary for us, so dear and precious for us as God. For absolutely every-

thing that we have now and that we have ever had, including even our very being—absolutely everything is a gift of God. The person who is the most needed, the most precious, the dearest of all for us is the one who usually first comes to our minds in the morning. As soon as we wake up in the morning, the thought of whoever or whatever is the most needed and dear to us wakes up as well. This always happens in the natural course of things. Therefore, it is always natural for our thoughts to turn first of all to the Lord God with some heartfelt appeal, such as "Glory to Thee, O Lord! Glory to Thee, O All-Merciful One!" We would be unworthy of the name of Christian if, waking from sleep, we were to open only our physical eyes, and not our spiritual ones, and were to think first of the earth and of earthly things, and not of the Lord God.

2. If the time at which you woke is the time at which or near which you should get up, then without any delay say, "In the name of the Father, and of the Son, and of the Holy Spirit," while making the sign of the cross. And then, "Lord Jesus Christ, Son of God, have mercy on me, a sinner."

3. Right after this, or at the same time, get out of bed. Getting out of bed quickly is often very unpleasant for our flesh, because our flesh, like a lazy servant, always likes to lie and sleep or to luxuriate and remain idle. Every single morning act against the base desires of your flesh. Let this opposition to the flesh be your first sacrifice to the Lord God. Among other reasons, quickly getting up in the morning is very beneficial

for the soul because (as all those who fervently strive for salvation have long observed) when we lie in bed for a long time after waking, impure tendencies very easily arise in our bodies, and impure thoughts and desires in our souls. Later in the day these easily cause the careless to fall into serious sins and into great danger of losing their salvation. But whoever bravely opposes the wishes of his flesh in the morning will resist temptations besetting him during the day and evening, even very serious ones. But if you have been watching after yourself to any degree, you already know this.

4. Having risen from bed, wash immediately, and having washed, dress immediately in a way that befits a respectable person. It is necessary to get dressed immediately like this in the morning, although there may be no one with us, because:

First, we never are completely alone; always and everywhere our Guardian Angel and the Lord God are with us. Our Guardian Angel, if we ourselves do not drive him away from us, is always with us, and the Lord God unquestionably is always with us by His very essence, because He is an omnipresent God. *For in him we live, and move, and have our being,* says the holy apostle (Acts 17:28).

Second, after having woken and washed, we should immediately stand before the Lord God with our morning prayers. And we would never dare to appear before even any of our lower-ranking earthly bosses without having dressed properly.

And finally, if you have dressed decently imme-diately after sleep, you will guard yourself from two dangers to which unfortunately very many people are subjected in our times, namely: from the danger of causing temptation for others and from the danger of becoming infected with the spirit of shamelessness. My friend, what can we expect in midday and evening from one who is shameless even in the morning?

5. After having washed and dressed, stand before the holy icons and say those morning prayers as spec-ified and in the order specified by the Holy Church, the interpreter and guardian of the path to salvation.

So that you may pray unimpeded, especially if you do not know how to read, learn by heart at least the beginning morning prayers. Is this difficult? And how could you not know by heart even the Lord's Prayer, that is, the prayer "Our Father, Who art in the heavens." Learn it! This is the most important prayer and most salvific for all occasions.

6. Because of our long familiarity with them, prayers learned by heart or read from a book are sometimes said without due attention to their con-tents, and we therefore are actually not praying, but just dreaming that we are praying. For this reason we may pray at times using words other than those of the prayers that are prepared and designated by the Holy Church. But when you pray this way, always carefully observe the following:

a.) Thank the Lord God that He preserved your life during the past night and is again giving you time for repentance and amendment of your life, for each new day is for us a new and not in the least bit deserved favor from God, because no new day automatically follows after night. Very many people, having quietly gone to sleep in the evening, have awakened not in this life, but in another one: eternity. Is it really that difficult for a person to lose his life? Sometimes even a mild fright can cause us to die. Not one night passes without many people dying during it. What preeminence do we have over those who have died in the past night? Could we not also die? Yes, we could, very easily. But who has preserved us from death, if not the All-good and All-merciful God, Who continuously awaits our repentance and amendment of our lives? He preserved us and has granted us a new day, that we might save our souls. So, can we not give thanks to the Lord God? Each morning thank Him with all your soul, like this, for example: "My Lord God and King! I thank Thee that during the the past night Thou hast preserved my life and that Thou hast again granted me time for repentance and amendment of my life. Many, many people have been deprived of their earthly lives in the past night. The day that is beginning is not an inevitable day in my life. It is beginning only because Thou art giving it to me because of Thine unspeakable mercy. I could easily have died in the past night. But Thou, O All-good One, hast saved me and hast given me a new day, that I might save my soul. I thank Thee with all my heart, O All-merciful One."

13

b.) Thank God for the other benefactions that you have received from Him. Thank Him that He created you, preserves you, redeemed you, brought you to the true faith, and in the true faith has provided you and continues to provide you with all means for salvation. All these benefactions are exceedingly great and deserving of unceasing and profound gratitude. Would you have felt the joy of life if the Lord God had not created you? Would you be alive now, if He had not preserved your life? What would happen to us if He had not redeemed us? How miserable we would be if He had not brought us into the true faith and in this way provided us with all the means for salvation! Even now, having the true faith and all the means for salvation, we are very miserable. How miserable, then, we would be without the true faith. Thank the Lord God incessantly and with all your soul, like this for example: "Lord God, My Father and King, I thank You that You have created me, have preserved me, have called me to the true faith, and in the true faith have provided and continue to provide me with all means for salvation. Would I feel the joy of life if You had not created me? Would I be alive now, if You had not preserved my life? What would have happened to me if You had not redeemed me? How miserable I would be if You had not brought me into the true faith and not provided me thus with all the means for salvation! I thank You with all my soul, All-Good and All-Merciful One."

c.) Thank the Lord God that, having provided you with all the means for salvation, He also unceasingly disposes you to use those means, and in spite of your frequent recalcitrance, in spite of the frequent grief that you cause Him, in spite of all your stubbornness, He does not punish you by depriving you of His great gift—life, but continues to call you and by various means disposes you to salvation. Oh, how long our bodies and souls would already be burning in the eternal fire of hell if the Lord God had not been so very merciful and longsuffering towards us. Thank the Lord with all your soul.

d.) Thank the Lord God that during the past night He deigned to strengthen your bodily powers and granted you the possibility to engage again in necessary and useful secular affairs. How many people because of various infirmities cannot acquire their daily subsistance. How many because of various illnesses cannot make the most necessary movements and constantly serve as a burden to others and to themselves. Thank the Lord God from all your heart for strengthening your bodily powers.

e.) After this pray with all your soul that the Lord God may forgive your innumerable sins, whether they were done in deed, intention, desire, or even only in thought. Never omit this prayer: you are always very sinful in the sight of the Lord God. In this regard not a single person should deceive himself. For in many things we offend all, the holy apostle says in the Spirit of God (James 3:2). And if we say that we have no sin, we deceive ourselves, and the truth is not in us, another holy apostle says in the same Spirit (I John 1:8).

f.) Pray that the Lord God may give you a firm, unalterable will to belong always and completely to Him, our constant Benefactor, from this day forward. This means to always consider the fulfilment of His will as our most important priority and to constantly try to live in complete accord with His holy will and therefore to try most zealously and above all else to discern His holy will, which in relation to us is basically always the same: our holiness (I Thess. 4:3), and the salvation of our souls (I Thess. 5:9; 2 Thess. 2:13).

7. That you may be able to keep yourself from sin more surely in the course of the coming day, try while it is still morning to think over everything that may happen to you during the day.

Try to examine what you are going to do and with whom you will spend time. What occasions of sin might you encounter? When and where? What opportunities for good might you encounter? When and where? Might you not have certain temptations, for example from your vainglory, from your pride, from your anger, and so on? Having examined everything this way, try at once to think over thoroughly how you can most easily and surely pass the whole day without sin, how to deal irreproachably with such and such a person, how to make good use of whatever opportunities for good we may encounter, how to avoid whatever occasions and temptations to sin or, if there is no possibility of avoiding them, how to handle oneself without harm in these occasions and temptations. For example, if you see that you will have to spend time with and work on something with a hot-tempered person, then you should try in advance to think of how to conduct yourself in his presence so meekly and politely that you will in no way provoke his anger, but remain at peace with him.

Without such a forearming of ourselves against sin it is impossible, or at least extremely difficult, to protect oneself from sin and to follow the Lord's teaching without faltering. Whoever does not make a firm resolution and effort each morning to preserve himself from sin during the coming day never diligently keeps himself from sin and little by little may finally abandon not only diligence, but the very desire and even the thought of obligation to preserve himself from sin. If the wick of a lampada is not adjusted and oil poured into the lampada every day, the lampada cannot burn constantly and soon will go out. My friend, do not forget this forearming against sin, which is very necessary every morning. When you really try to preserve yourself from every sin and keep to a God-pleasing and holy life, then you will soon see for yourself the great need and salutary effects of this forearming.

8. So that you may even more easily and securely lead a holy life, pray to the Lord God that He may bless to grant you constant consciousness and zeal to avoid the occasions of sin, and especially of that sin to which you are most inclined by nature or habit. Because such a sin strongly induces each of us to satisfy its demand, and all of us who are still not fully

devoted to God usually satisfy it so willingly that when we encounter obstacles to fulfilling it, we try with all our strength to eliminate those obstacles and to clear the way to satisfy that sin unhindered and, as much as possible, without delay. It is very difficult for a person to protect himself from such a sin, and our age-old enemy attacks us from nowhere so often, so insolently, and so confidently as from the direction of our favorite, habitual sin. Pray with all your soul.

9. Having thus examined and thought over everything necessary for protecting yourself from sin and anchoring yourself in a God-pleasing life, again pray in your heart to the Lord God that He may strengthen your will and your powers and not allow you to weaken, as you have so often weakened before. Without such a prayer expressed in these or other words, do not on any day engage in any matter for any reason, except perhaps a reason completely out of your control. How can we set about any matter without the blessing of God? Without God's blessing all our labors are in vain. But God's blessing, like every gift of God, is obtained only by prayer (James 1:17). True, the Lord God in His infinite goodness often gives success in their affairs also to people who do not pray or even are impious. Do not take mind of this. When this thought comes to mind, think immediately about the fearsome fate of the rich man mentioned in the Gospel, who loved to make merry sumptuously every day (Luke 16:19--32). In his life he had success in everything, never felt the slightest

18

need, and had all the means for satisfying his sensual passions and always satisfied them fully. But this way of life, after his death, plunged him into the torments of hell. And when he, being horribly tormented in the flames, wretchedly implored Abraham for relief of his torments, he was refused, and the refusal consisted of words that the fortunate of this world should all remember keenly every minute. The refusal was as follows: *Son, remember that thou in thy lifetime receivedst thy good things . . . but now . . . thou art tormented* (Luke 16:25).

10. One should pray like this especially in the morning, and one should make such a resolution and take such prudent measures in the morning. No other time is so appropriate for prayer and for all good undertakings as the morning, because at no other time is a person so capable of prayer, or of undertaking business, or of reflection as in the morning. In the morning, his thoughts are much less constricted, his heart is purer, and he can contain himself much more easily than at any another time. In the morning the necessities of life are not yet bothering us, the passions are still sleeping, and the very nature surrounding us disposes us to a serious and reflective state. With the passing of morning the passions awaken, everyday needs appear and stir up cares, a person begins work and toils like a slave who must always eat bread in the sweat of [his] face. My friend, spend the morning in prayer and in the holy guidance of your life. Put a high value on the morning of every day. Be

wise, for the Spirit of God portrays the behavior of a wise man thus: He will give his heart to resort early to the Lord that made him, and will pray before the most High (Ecclesiasticus 39:5).

11. After praying thus, sit down and in reverence towards the Lord God unhurriedly and thoroughly consider how you should conduct yourself during the coming day in relation to the Lord God, to your neighbors, and to your particular position in the world. And if on some mornings something hinders you from engaging in such reflection, then in any case always do it every Sunday and holy day morning: on these days nothing can and should be a hindrance for you. Our flesh, injured by the ancestral sin, is in close touch with our age-old enemy, the devil, and together with him continually tries to erase our Christian duties from our memory and to revive in their place various rules of the world and, at the same time or even before, to revive various means of satisfying its passions. To our misfortune, they succeed very often and very easily. Do not listen to these pernicious teachers, and by all means possible try each morning to remind yourself of your spiritual obligations, as they are laid on you by the Lord God, and again make the firm resolution to fulfil them more exactly and diligently.

HOW SHOULD WE CONDUCT OURSELVES IN RELATION TO THE LORD GOD?

Our Lord Jesus Christ Himself gave us the answer to that question: *Thou shalt love the Lord thy God with all thy heart, and with all thy soul, and with all thy strength, and with all thy mind; and thy neighbour as thyself* (Luke 10:27).

What does love God mean? Without any doubt, to love God means to be devoted to God.

What does to "love God with all our hearts, with all our souls, with all our mind, and with all our strength" mean? This means to be steadfastly devoted to God with our whole hearts and souls; that is, with all the strength and fullness of love that is possible for the human heart, not sharing our love in the same measure with any other being, however beloved, needed, and dear that being may be to us.

To love God with all thy heart, and so forth, means to think more often and more readily about God and about what is pleasing to God, because in general it is an attribute of the love of our heart that the one whom we sincerely love is constantly with us in our thoughts. We are often separated from the one we love, but are always with that one in our thoughts: looking at, listening to, and speaking with him or her.

To love God with all thy heart means to speak about the Lord God as often, as long, and as readily as we can. Because it is an attribute of the love of our heart that we speak as often, as long, and as willingly as possible about whomever we sincerely love, for you speak of whatever lies deepest in your heart: *for out of the abundance of the heart the mouth speaketh* (Matt. 12:34).

To love God with all thy heart means to try to the greatest extent possible to learn the will of God, or that which is pleasing to God and that which offends Him, and then as readily, diligently, and joyfully as possible to do what is pleasing to the Lord God, and as attentively and thoughtfully as we can to avoid what offends Him. For it is an attribute of the love of our heart that we try to the greatest extent possible to know the will of whomever we sincerely love and to fulfill it with all diligence and pleasure, no matter how difficult that may be.

To love God with all thy heart means to fulfill the will of God readily and with joy, even when this is sure to demand great self-sacrifice of us. For it is an attribute of the love of the human heart that we try to fulfill the will of whomever we sincerely love, regardless of any obstacles, difficulties, or unpleasantness, to fulfill it regardless even of clear danger to our lives. Love overcomes all obstacles; for it, everything difficult is easy, everything unpleasant is pleasant, and everything heavy is light.

To love God with all thy heart means to glorify the Lord God with the greatest zeal and to try with all our power to put a stop to or prevent anything that impugns His glory. For it is always an attribute of our love that we everywhere praise whomever we sincerely love and at any unpleasant mention of our beloved we try to our utmost to defend the honor of our beloved and his or her good name. For we are always gratified when our beloved is held in respect by all and displeased when he or she is not loved and not respected.

Such should be our love for the Lord God, and it is entirely fitting that we should love Him with all the fullness of our love.

1. We naturally love everything beautiful even in created beings, even though we know that everything beautiful in created beings is often transitory and

always imperfect. We sincerely love the goodness of soul in a person, notwithstanding that such goodness is often combined in him with not a few weaknesses or even vices. But the Lord God is indescribable beauty, eternal beauty, never ceasing and never changing, as well as being the single Cause of all created beauty. The Lord God has goodness of heart the like of which is not found in any creature of God, neither on earth, nor in heaven. The goodness in everyone else's heart is there only because the Lord God bestowed it in His goodness. In short, God is an all-perfect being. How could we not love God with all the fullness of our love?

2. The Lord God bestowed the gift of life upon us. From Him we received a rational soul able to think, judge, and understand. From Him we received a heart able to love and feel pleasure from love. From Him we received the means to keep all of our mental and bodily powers in a proper state of health. Therefore, our whole soul with all its powers belongs entirely to God. How could we not love God with all the fullness of our love? What could be more beloved for us than the Creator, Who bestowed the gift of life upon us, the ability to think, judge, understand, love, feel pleasure from love, and feel joy, and Who in addition has bestowed on us the means to keep all of these gifts of His in a proper state of strength and health?

3. We are surrounded by air, which we breathe and without which our life would be impossible. We are everywhere supplied with water, which is just as

necessary for us as air is. We are placed on the earth, which yields to us every kind of food necessary for the maintenance and preservation of our life, and without which we would have nowhere to set our feet. We are illuminated by light, without which we could not obtain anything pleasant, or necessary for life, even if everything we needed were ready and close to us. We have fire, with which we can warm ourselves during very cold weather and with which we cook the food that we need. In short, we have everything needed not only for our life, but even for our pleasure. And all this is a gift of the Lord God. How could we not love God with our whole soul and our whole heart?

4. We have a father, a mother, brothers, sisters, relatives, benefactors, friends, and other people who are close to us. How much joy and consolation they bring us! But we should have none of them, if the Lord God had not willed to give them to us. Even we ourselves should not exist if the the kindness of God had not allowed it. We have all of this only by the mercy of God. How could we not love the Lord God with all the fullness of our love?

5. We have some property: the house in which we live, the food and drink by which we maintain and continue life, the clothing with which we cover our nakedness and protect it from the harmful effects of bad weather. But all of this is a gift from God. Could we have a house, food, clothing, and countless other necessities and conveniences of life if the Lord God had not willed to create the materials from which all

these things are made? And even if we had the materials, could we have all of these things if the Lord God had not deigned to bestow upon us a mind and hands for the production of everything that we need? No, we could not. How can we not love with all the fulness of our love God, Who serves as our benefactor so much and so continually?!

6. After their creation, the Lord God visited the the first humans, our ancestors, in the garden of Eden (Genesis 2:15), where they found complete satisfaction in all things. But their subsequent fall not only deprived them and us of the Garden of Eden, but also rendered them and us predisposed to sin, illness, and death. The entire human race, which descends from our first parents, was and is to a greater or lesser extent wilful, proud, self-seeking, unloving, envious, deceitful, malicious, vengeful, and more. In such a condition there was no way that it could recover its original blessed state. For, on the one hand, the Lord God, like the purest light (I John 1:5), could not have contact with it, which by its sins had become darkness (Ephesians 5:8), because light does not consort with darkness (II Cor. 6:14), but only God is the source of light (Ps. 35: 10) or of blessedness. On the other hand, the human race in the depravity of its heart could commit only sin, and sin can cause only evil and misfortune for it. For the Spirit of God describes sin thus: the teeth thereof are as the teeth of a lion, slaying the souls of men. *All iniquity is as a two edged sword, the wounds whereof cannot be healed*(Ecclus. 21: 2-3). But the Lord God did not

abandon the human race even in this condition, which is an abomination to Him. He did not destroy it but continued and still continues to maintain its existence, supplying it with everything necessary for life. He gave the human race His law, which pointed it towards the good and promised it prosperity (Deut. 5:29). But as man in his foolishness and depravity neither loved nor fulfilled the law given him, God tried repeatedly, by means of His Prophets and in many other ways, to instruct him, correct him, and guide him to the fulfilment of His law. But none of these steps that God took to correct the human race succeeded in correcting it, and it only gave itself over more and more to sin and sank into iniquity. Therefore God, being filled with love, was gracious enough to send us His Only-begotten Son--our God--in order to open the possibility, in the very face of impossibility, of making the human race blessed. His eternal Son was born on earth, like us, was brought up, was hungry and thirsty and worked day and night to teach men the way of salvation, to save them from the misfortune that oppresses them, but this inexpressibly merciful Son of God was tortured and killed on a cross by these same men. Such horrifying ingratitude demanded the sternest punishment for mankind. But the Lord repaid such ingratitude only with the most abundant grace. The Son of God, having risen from the dead, sent the All-Holy Spirit to the human race for its enlightenment, founded the Holy Church, established the Holy Mysteries, established the priesthood, to which He gave the right to absolve sins for all those who truly repent, and so on. If we give this the proper attention, it is impossible not to see that God truly is love, as the holy Apostle calls Him (I John 4:16), filled with love for the human race (John 3:16), and that therefore the first commandment of God, the commandment to love God with all our minds and all our souls, is a commandment absolutely obligatory for all of us. Therefore, if any of us reveals even the slightest of doubts that this commandment is absolutely obligatory for all of us, then he would openly show that he has neither a human mind nor a human heart, that he has lost his human dignity and has descended to a level lower than that of the irrational beasts, because the irrational beasts, as we all know, usually greatly love their benefactors, who are incomparably inferior to God.

7. There is no being who could love us more than the Lord God, and we always love the one who loves us and does good to us. Therefore, to love God with our whole heart and our whole soul should be the very first need of every person's heart, especially since love is the most pleasant feeling for all of us. But as many people, because of error, recklessness, or extreme depravity, do not feel this necessity and do not try to satisfy it, the Lord God gave us the commandment to love Him with our whole hearts and our whole souls not because our love could somehow increase His blessedness or majesty, but because He greatly desires to make us blessed, and without our love for Him from our whole souls and from our whole hearts,

we cannot be blessed. "The scarcity of love for God in our souls is the most intolerable of all evils," says St. Basil the Great. The commandment given us by the Lord God to love Him with all our souls and all our hearts is clear proof, on the one hand, that God greatly desires our salvation and blessedness and, on the other, of our deep fall, vile coarsening, and great depravity.

But unfortunately, we see among people everywhere those in whom love for God is extremely weak or even negligible. This is manifestly shown in their unchanging coldness towards everything Divine, disdain for God's churches and services, disrespect for sacred things, indifference both towards everything pleasing and agreeable to God and towards what is displeasing and offensive to Him. Some people almost never talk about God, and do not even like to talk about Him; they almost never remember God, and remembering Him causes them discontent or even irritation; they not only do not live according to God's commandments, as if these did not exist and they were not in the least obliged to live by them, but they do not even want to know whether there are Divine commandments and what they require.

Friend, examine yourself to see if you are such a person, and if you are, then quickly offer the Lord God your heartfelt repentance and immediately, with intense prayer to the Lord and Savior of the world, begin to amend your life. Make no tarrying to turn to the Lord, and put not off from day to day, the Wise one says to the sinner (Ecclus. 5:7). He says exactly the same thing to you as well. Look at yourself: you have nothing of your own, but everything belongs to God, and you yourself are not your own, but also belong to God. How can you be so blind, imprudent, and foolish not to love the Lord God with your whole soul and with your whole heart?

HOW SHOULD WE CONDUCT OURSELVES IN RELATIONSHIP TO OTHER PEOPLE?

The answer to this question is given by the Lord Himself: Love thy neighbor (Luke 10:27). The Lord Jesus Christ very categorically demands that we love one another. While giving His last instructions to His Disciples before His suffering, He often, and with great force, entrusted them with this love, namely: *This is My Commandment, That ye love one another* (John 15:17). *A new commandment I give you, That ye love one another...* (John 13:34). This is precisely what all of the apostles oblige us to do. The holy Apostle Peter, together with all the other apostles, commanded us to love. St. Peter writes: *...See that ye love one another with a pure heart fervently* (I Peter 1:22). St. John the Theologian writes: *Beloved, let us love one another* (I John 3:11; John 5). *And this is His commandment, That we should believe on the name of His Son Jesus Christ, and love one another, as He gave us commandment* (I John 3:23). St. Paul says: *Walk in love* (Eph. 5:2). *...For ye yourselves are taught of God to love one another* (I Thess. 4:9). The holy Apostle James writes: *the royal law according to the Scriptures* [is], *Thou shalt love thy neighbor as thyself...* (James 2:8).

The measure of this love is clearly defined by the Lord Himself. He demands that we all love our neighbor as ourselves, for He said: *Thou shalt love thy neighbor as thyself* (Luke 10:27). *...Whatsoever ye would that men should do to you, do ye even so to them* (Matthew 7:12). This is exactly what all the holy apostles said. Therefore my reader, take note and fulfill the following instructions.

1. You want the best for yourself and are satisfied when everything works out for the best. On the other hand you are not pleased when for some reasons things fail. Therefore wish the best for all your neighbors: rejoice when they are happy and commiserate when they fall into misfortune.

2. It is unpleasant when people react to you poorly and suspect you of some evil doing. Therefore do not speak poorly of anyone, and without sufficient

cause do not be suspicious of anyone. *Love thinketh no evil* (I Cor. 13:5).

3. It is pleasant for you when people speak well of you. Therefore you should speak well of all your neighbors. be especially careful not to slander your neighbor. Slander is the work of Satan, let it belong to him alone (Rev. 12:10). You speak only good of your neighbor.

4. When someone speaks poorly about someone outside your circle, try, if at all possible, to defend or excuse him. Besides this, never repeat that which you have heard. For it frequently happens that things are said about people because of malice or out of revenge, and to repeat that which was said can cause enmity. Enmity is described in the Word of God as one of those vices which can prevent one from entering the Kingdom of Heaven (Gal. 5:20).

5. It is unpleasant for you when people divulge your shortcomings and especially your vices. Therefore when you see the weaknesses and vices of others, do not announce them to everyone for *Charity...beareth all things,...endureth all things* (I Cor. 13:4-7). Look for the right occasion and lovingly point out the weaknesses and vices you noticed; incline the person to correct himself. After a time, if you see that the vices you noticed do not scandalize others, then you yourself cease from mentioning them. If possible tell them to a person (like a priest) who is assigned to correct and check them and protect others from temptation and harm. To tempt others is a terrible sin (Matt. 18:6).

You do not like it when others treat you roughly and offend you in some way. Therefore you should treat everyone kindly without exception. Be especially careful not to use swear words or offensive ones. If it so happens that someone treats you crudely, angrily, and says unpleasant things to you, then answer him meekly, for, *A soft answer turneth away wrath* (Prov. 15:1). If it happens that because of an offence you became angry with your neighbor, then say nothing, for immediately your anger will flame up, and in an impassioned state you are likely to consider it necessary to say something that later sorely regret, but will be incapable of correcting. While angry say nothing but wait until you have completely calmed down. If your neighbor is for some reason very angry with you, do not attempt to talk him out of it, even if it seems very necessary, for while he is in the heat of anger the passion is in control of him and not his reason, therefore you must not try to dissuade him—it is impossible to speak convincingly to someone out of his mind, your words will only make him more angry and force him to do something possibly harmful to you.

7. You are pleased when people help you when you are in need. Therefore strive yourself, as much as you can, to help your neighbor in all of his needs. *For alms* (all good deeds) *doth deliver from death, and shall purge away all sin. Those that exercise alms and righteousness shall be filled with life* (Tobit 12:9), the Word of God tells us. Here we must follow a special rule. Namely:

a) We must, before helping other people help those whom God's foresight has united us with, i.e., parents, relatives, authorities, benefactors, those under our authority, and fellow believers. St. Paul says concerning the first group, *But if any provide not for those of his own house, he hath denied the Faith, and is worse than an infidel* (I Tim. 5:8). Concerning fellow believers the Apostle teaches: *As we have therefore opportunity, let us do good unto all men, especially unto them who are of the household of Faith.* (Gal. 6:10).

b) Among the above, before others, come to the assistance of those who are especially in need, that is the ill and disabled. Even if you cannot give them what they specifically need, then at least visit them, serve them in some way, and comfort them. Act in this way even if they are totally ungrateful to you, for *Love does not seek its own* (I Cor. 13:5), and the Lord will reward you.

8) Having assisted those among your living neighbors, do not deny those among your departed neighbors. Pray for all the departed, and especially for those who died suddenly and without proper preparation, and while still in serious sins. Remember them more often and offer what alms you can for their salvation. Many of our departed neighbors, especially those who reposed without proper preparation, need our help incomparably more than those among the living who are extremely impoverished, because the reposed are now incapable of helping themselves. Only we the living can offer help.

9) Our love for ourselves can be and , unfortunately, often is truly misplaced. How many people desire and strive for earthly goods, great honor, respect, prosperity. Therefore our Lord Jesus Christ was so pleased to place a specific condition on our love for our neighbor; He commanded that we should love our neighbor as He loved us. *This is My commandment, That ye love one another, as I have loved you* (John 15:12). The Lord Jesus Christ so loved us, the faithful, His Church, that He *gave Himself for it; That He might sanctify it... That He might present it to Himself... not having spot, or wrinkle, or any such thing; but that it should be holy and without blemish* (Eph. 5:25-27). He strove and strives to create in all of us firm faith in God the Father and in Himself (John 3:16), to offer us a true knowledge of God (John 1:18; 17:3), to inspire us to love Him (John 17:26), to lovingly and zealously fulfill the commandments of God (John 14:21, 23, 24) and to lead us to eternal life (John 3:16).

Therefore each of us who sincerely loves himself should in every way possible strive to acquire firm faith in the Lord God, true knowledge of Him, heartfelt love for Him and the most zealous desire to fulfill His commandments. Thus we should also act in relationship to our neighbor so that he might acquire firm faith in the Lord God, true knowledge of Him, acquire love for Him, zealously striving to fulfill His commandments and thus continually grow towards eternal blessedness. Every one of us should in every way possible inspire our neighbor to care for the salvation of his soul, to support and increase this concern by whatever means possible. None of us should dare say: "What do I have to do with the quality of my neighbor's life?" Quite the opposite, each of us, when we notice that a Christian is behaving in an improper way, should look for the right time in order to privately and with love bring him to his senses and direct him on the right path of salvation. *Now we exhort you* (not just ask), *brethren, warn them that are unruly* (I Thess. 5:14).

In order to assist our neighbor spiritually we should strive much more earnestly than to help him physically. Physical help must be offered in such a way that it more or less contributes to the spiritual perfection of our neighbor and to his salvation. The spiritual need of our neighbor is incomparably more important than any of his physical needs. And to give spiritual assistance is often much more difficult than to give physical because, as a rule, people usually respond for physical assistance with gratitude, but to spiritual, almost never, and it is not unusual for them to repay us with hatred and even vengeance.

10) As in offering physical help, in offering spiritual help we must also follow a special rule mainly: before helping others we should heed the needs of people that God's Providence has closely bound us with, such as our children, relatives, friends, benefactors, employees. He who strives to instruct, correct and awaken the conscience in strangers while his own

children or employees run out of control and fall into sins and error, does not fulfill the commandment of love for his neighbor. He is not a friend to his neighbor but an enemy, one who is at times extremely harmful and destructive.

11) If the opportunity arises we should never refuse physical and especially spiritual help to the depraved, to foreigners, non-orthodox, heretics, atheists, and enemies, for all of them, no matter what their orientation or disposition, are human, all created by the Creator, all with an immortal soul and in the likeness of God. They are all redeemed by the priceless Blood of Jesus Christ and therefore all children of the Heavenly Father, all redeemed by Christ and all co-inheritors of the one, eternal, all-blessed Kingdom of God. Therefore we should show love to all people. People who are depraved, heretics, and atheists, all are in the greatest need of our spiritual aid, especially our prayers and our example to them. Concerning our enemies there is the clear commandment of the Lord: *But I say unto you, Love your enemies, bless them that curse you, do good to them that hate you, and pray for them which despitefully use you, and persecute you* (Matt. 5:44). There can be no contradiction here, for the Apostle John makes it clear to us that: *Whoever hateth his brother is a murderer* (John 3:15).

This is how we should love our neighbor. If we were filled with love for all our neighbors we would be perfectly happy. Then there would not be such unhappiness on earth and our life would be like the

38

life of our ancestors in blissful paradise. Let us zeal-ously fulfill the Lord's commandments of love for our neighbor, and in every way possible strive to bring our lives closer to that of our ancestors in paradise!

HOW SHOULD WE CONDUCT OURSELVES IN SOME OF THE MOST COMMON SITUATIONS OF LIFE?

In the course of our lives we usually find that our situations change. The situations in which people find themselves in the present life are innumerable. Therefore, it is impossible to survey all situations in human life.

I want to direct attention only to our most common situations in life and show how we should conduct ourselves in them.

1. How to Conduct Ourselves in Happiness

1. When you are happy, that is, when everything in life is going according to your wishes: you
are healthy, your wife, your children, and your family is healthy, your neighbors like you, all your affairs
are going well, you are satisfied and do not feel need,
then every morning and every evening thank the
Lord God from your whole soul for all of this and be
very careful not to be ungrateful to Him. Everyone
recognizes as vile those who are ungrateful to other
people; even more so should we acknowledge as vile
those who are ungrateful to the Lord God. The holy
Apostle numbers the ingratitude of people among the
vices of the people of the last time (II Timothy 3:2),
that is, of the most depraved time.

2. In using your earthly well-being with gratitude,
never forget that the Lord God grants us to live hap-
pily on earth not so that we might only rejoice and
be glad, but so that we, feeling the goodness of God,
might be grateful to the Lord God, that is, do nothing displeasing to Him, and if we were to do something displeasing to Him, we should offer repentance, for "the goodness of God leadeth thee," says
the holy Apostle to the fortunate of the world, not
to amusements and a self-willed life, but to repentance (Romans 2:3,4). "God shows you His mercy so
that you will stop sinning. If you do not stop sinning,
then your punishment will be terrible," says St. John
Chrysostom. Whoever forgets about this purpose of
God's goodness concerning earthly blessings becomes

comfortably attached to earthly prosperity with all his heart and, indulging only his worldly passions, forgets God and forgets eternal blessedness and his soul. And what will happen to his soul? Friend, consider! Its fate will be terrible!

3. Therefore, in making use of earthly well-being, avoid becoming attached to it in your heart; that is, do not fall in love with the joys and comforts that your earthly well-being can and does afford you. Your heart should cleave completely only to the Lord God. Never forget His words, filled with love, spoken through the Most wise Solomon: *give me, son, your heart* (Proverbs 23:26). Do not forget: be obedient. All the joys and comforts of your earthly well-being are worldly joys and comforts, and the holy apostle absolutely forbids us to love the world and that which is in it, because whoever loves the world lacks what is central and most necessary for true well-being, namely love for the Lord God, for *if any man love the world, the love of the Father is not in him,* according to the holy apostle (I John 2:15).

4. So that it may be easier to protect yourself from love of the joys and comforts of your earthly well-being, act as the saints acted. While making use of earthly blessings, they ceaselessly remembered and sighed for the heavenly blessings. You should act that way too. Accustom yourself to remember heavenly bliss as often as possible and say, "Lord, if it is so good for me under your shelter even on earth, what will it be like in heaven? Thy kingdom come." Or

42

"Lord, You gladden me so much on earth. Deprive me not of Thy heavenly joy." Or "Lord, how much consolation Your boundless goodness gives my soul. Do not allow it in this consolation somehow to fall asleep in sin." Or, "O Lord, how great is your goodness to me, and how foolish I am. How little I love You. What little zeal I have to root out of myself various vices, but especially my favorite sin. Enlighten me. Awaken me. Set me on the path of salvation. Have mercy on me and save me."

5. When you feel that, in making use of your earthly well-being, you lose your bearings somewhat, then pray with all your soul to the Lord God, that He might have the kindness to draw your heart more firmly to Himself and that He might prefer to deprive you of all your well-being if it threatened to draw your heart away from Him and destroy your soul; for it is incomparably better to endure on earth not only every kind of deprivation, but even the worst tortures, than to lose God and to suffer eternally.

2. How to Conduct Ourselves in Misfortune

1. When you are struck by some kind of misfortune: infamy, persecution, poverty, domestic turmoil, and so on, whether from other people, or from the circumstances of your life, or from the circumstances of nature, never give yourself over to immoderate sorrow, fear, grumbling, or despair, because St. Basil the Great says that the Most Wise and All-Good Master sends us each earthly misfortune for our benefit and

43

precisely *that we might be partakers of his holiness,* as the holy Apostle affirms (Heb. 12:10).

2. On the contrary, when any misfortune befalls you, and you feel guilty of something, then immediately imagine the Lord Jesus Christ on the cross and cry out to Him with all your heart, "All-Merciful Lord, double, triple, or increase my grief tenfold, but do not allow me to perish in sin. What do all my temporary misfortunes matter, compared to eternal torments?" Or, "My Lord and God! You suffered incomparably more for me than I can suffer, but You, being Most Pure, suffered completely innocently and suffered moreover without the slightest complaint or ill will, but I have merited much more misfortune, so can I grumble at my present misfortune? Have mercy on me. Teach me. Grant me zeal to correct myself, and strengthen me in this zeal. Have mercy on me and save me."

If, when misfortune befalls you, you feel that you are innocent, thank the Lord God with all your heart that He, as we must think without any doubt, desires by the misfortune sent you or permitted for you to preserve you from something disastrous for the salvation of your soul, "because joy makes the soul frivolous, haughty, and inconstant," says Chrysostom. In the present life, in times of good fortune, we all give ourselves over very easily to vainglory, pride, luxury, love of sensual pleasure, and other vices, so that often it is very difficult to teach us and bring us into true self-awareness while our good fortune continues. Therefore the holy Apostle says, *we must through much*

44

tribulation enter into the kingdom of God (Acts 14:22). Imagining this, say to the Lord God: "My Creator and Savior! You Yourself came to earth not for joy, but for suffering, and told us, *Remember the word that I said unto you, The servant is not greater than his lord* (John 15:20). I will endure everything to which Your right hand may subject me. It is all-good, and what else can I expect from it but true good for my soul? Thy will be done in all things. Have the kindness to fortify me, so that I, not forgetting You and my soul, will remain completely grateful and submissive towards Your every command, as once did Your devoted servant Job" (Job 1: 13-22).

Act this way, no matter whence your misfortune may come: from hostile people or from the elements, from wild animals or from livestock, and so on, because your misfortune really comes not from them, but from God. Nothing ever happens to us without God's will or without His consent. *God is king of all the earth,* the holy prophet says (Psalms 46:7). *There shall not an hair of your head perish* without the will of your Father, the Lord Himself tells us (Luke 21:18). All the saints of all time understood it this way. When our primordial enemy took from the much-suffering Job his property and his children, he did not say "the devil took this away from me"; he said, *The Lord gave, and the Lord hath taken away* (Job 1:21). Take note of this and act this way too. Patience is a most salvific quality. *Behold, we count them happy which endure,* the holy apostle says (James 5:11).

3. How to Conduct Ourselves in Wealth

If you are rich, that is, if you have much more than you need for the basic requirements of your life:

1. Never think, as many foolish people among the rich do, that you owe your wealth to your intelligence, your cleverness, or your energy. Although you, perhaps, really are intelligent, clever, and energetic, never attribute the acquisition of your wealth only to these attributes; for consider: who gave you your intelligence? Who gave and gives you health and strength, so that you can work? Who blesses your labors with the success you desire, while many other people no less intelligent and hardworking than you are hardly able to get their daily piece of bread? And who looks after your wealth, which you could lose at any moment from any number of circumstances? Is it not God, your Creator, Who does this? Remember the word of the Spirit of God, *The Lord. . . maketh rich* (1 Kings 2:7) and so do not take pride in your wealth, but be humble when you are rich, consider it a gift from God, and fervently thank the Lord God for it.

2. When you pray, never in your prayer ask the Lord God for permanent continuation of your earthly plenty, and especially do not ask for increase of wealth, because, although the Lord God does give wealth to some people, nowhere is it commanded for us to ask for wealth, but it is said that even when, so to speak, it "flows in" to us by itself, we should *set not [our] hearts thereon* (Psalm 61: 11).

3. Do not cling to wealth with your heart, lest it begin to rule your heart and you become its slave, but hold your heart in relationship to it in such a way that you would be able to get along comfortably without it, as soon as it is the Lord God's will to take your wealth from you. If you become attached to wealth, it will immediately draw you towards countless vices and put you in an extremely dangerous state of soul. Jesus Christ says that wealth can be very perilous for the soul: *a rich man shall hardly enter into the kingdom of heaven* (Matt. 19:23), and *they that will be rich fall into many foolish and hurtful lusts, which drown men in destruction and perdition,* as the holy Apostle says (I Tim. 6:9).

In making use of wealth, beware especially of acting as did the foolish rich man that the Lord mentioned in the Gospel (Luke 16:19 and following). While he himself made merry sumptuously, he preferred to give even the crumbs from his table to dogs, rather than to the poor man wasting away from hunger at the doors to his house. After his death, that rich man immediately found himself in hell (Luke 16:23) and will burn there eternally, not receiving even a drop of water from anywhere to cool his tongue (Luke 16: 25,26).

4. How to Conduct Ourselves in Poverty

If you are poor, that is, if you are hard-working and in spite of all your labors you barely get enough to provide daily bread for you and your children, then bear your poverty with equanimity. Bear this difficulty with equanimity until the time that it is pleasing to the Lord God to take it from you; bear it to death itself, if it is pleasing to Him. Always be cheerful, do not grief, do not grumble, and especially do not become despondent, no matter how your poverty deepens and how long it lasts. Especially avoid using any kind of improper means that are contrary to God's will to rescue yourself from poverty. Not only should you not use any kind of theft, any kind of deception, forced seizures of property, and so forth, but except in the most unavoidable extremes, do not even ask for alms. *Lead not a beggar's life; for better it is to die than to beg,* teaches the Wise one (Ecclesiasticus 40:28). So that you may be able to bear up better in this disposition of soul, do the following:

1. Continuously remember the words of the Holy Spirit, *The Lord maketh poor* (I Sam. 2:7). But when the Lord God places any of us in some condition, He places him in that condition because that person can always be saved much more easily in the condition appointed him. Because the Lord God has no other desire concerning us except that we be saved (I Tim. 2:4), whatever He may do with us He does to facilitate our salvation.

2. Never forget that the Lord God never will lay upon you a burden greater than you can bear (I Cor. 10:13), and that He is always near you to offer you His aid (Matthew 28:20). He will never forget you or leave you. No mother can ever forget the off-

spring of her womb; even less can He forget you, as He Himself affirms through the holy prophet: *yea, a woman may forget the son of her womb, yet will I not forget thee* (Isaias 49:15). Thus, if you in your poverty are not fainthearted, the Lord God will without fail lead you to salvation--to eternal bliss.

3. As often as possible, remember the earthly poverty of our Savior. He is God; everything is His: both what is in the heavens, and what is on earth, in the earth, and beneath the earth, but He lived on earth in complete poverty, as He Himself said, *foxes have holes, and birds of the air have nests; but the Son of man hath not where to lay his head* (Luke 9:58). For what purpose did He live so poorly? Of course, not for any other purpose than to incline all of us to accept poverty with equanimity and to be satisfied with what is most necessary for sustaining life; for poverty, as St. John Chrysostom says, leads to piety more easily than wealth.

4. Remember often the much-suffering Job, whom the holy Apostle James holds up as an example of patience. Job was utterly impoverished. All his flocks, all his slaves, all his children had been taken away from him, and he said, *Naked came I out of my mother's womb, and naked shall I return thither: the Lord gave, and the Lord hath taken away; as it seemed good unto the Lord, so hath it come to pass: blessed be the name of the Lord* (Job 1:21). Even when he had been struck by a malignant and excruciating disease and when even his closest friends and his wife mocked

him--even then he did not lose his patience, but said placidly to everyone, *What? shall we receive good at the hand of God, and shall we not receive [endure] evil?* (Job 2:10).

5. Call to mind as often as possible that the majority of the saints spent their lives in poverty. The holy apostle says of the majority of the saints of the Old Testament that they *wandered about in sheepskins and goatskins; being destitute, afflicted, tormented; (Of whom the world was not worthy:) they wandered in deserts, and in mountains, and in dens and caves of the earth* (Hebr. 11:37,38). In the New Testament, as is known, all the best people passed their lives in the greatest poverty: all the holy apostles, all the first bishops, all the first priests, all the ancient desert-dwellers. Of the last, many completely lacked clothing to cover their nakedness and, like the wild animals, lived only on green plants.

6. If in your poverty some other burdens oppress you, again do not lose your spirits, but comfort yourself with holy thoughts. For example, people hate you or despise you. Think: "What does it matter? My Lord and Savior was God, but they hated and despised even Him. He was not at all diminished because of this. Should I not endure hatred and scorn, when the Lord also says, *Blessed are ye, when men shall hate you* (Luke 6:22)." Do they oppress you and insult you? Think: "What does it matter? Who did they oppress and insult more than the Lord Himself? Finally, they oppressed and insulted Him

to the point that they crucified Him. But what did He lose because of this? For His patience God the Father exalted Him to such a degree that at His name should bow *every knee. . . of things in heaven, and things in earth, and things under the earth* (Philip. 2:10)." Think further: "If people do not despise and humiliate someone, how can that person get practice in humility? If they do not insult him, how can he learn patience, meekness, and so forth?"

7. Finally, think more often about the heavenly blessings, which you will surely enjoy if you patiently endure your poverty to the end. The pauper mentioned by the Lord in the Gospel was on earth poor as almost no one else, and how glorious was the end of his life. The angels took and carried his soul to the bosom of Abraham. There his condition was suddenly changed. He had not had the slightest joy during his entire life, but now he is delighting in the greatest joys, continuous and eternal. The same will happen also with you: you will not have to endure necessity always; you will not suffer always; a reward is being prepared for you, and the reward for the faithful in heaven cannot compare with any of our earthly sorrows. The holy Apostle says, *the sufferings of this present time are not worthy to be compared with the glory which shall be revealed in us* (Rom. 8:18). *Eye hath not seen, nor ear heard, neither have entered into the heart of man, the things which God hath prepared for them that love him* (I Cor. 2:9).

5. How to Conduct Ourselves When People Praise Us

When people praise you, be very circumspect, because then you are in a dangerous situation.

1. Many people do not know the true value of things and of actions, and therefore they value and praise things that in the sight of the Lord God and of sensible people are worth nothing. And because praise is pleasing to our self-esteem and vainglory, and self-esteem and vainglory are gullible, we eagerly accept another's false praise as true praise, put a halt to seeking perfection, become more imperfect, die unreformed, and perish. Therefore, consider as impartially as possible whether what others praise in you deserves praise from the Lord and from prudent people, because only that which is worthy of praise from the Lord God and from people devoted to Him should be important for us. What does praise from people matter, when we are unworthy of praise from the Lord God?

2. People who want to deceive us in something or get from us some earthly benefit always approach us with obsequiousness, that is, with some degree of praise for us. They often quite intentionally praise in us something that we do not at all have, or that we do have, but not yet at such a high degree to justify so much praise. And if we are a bit puffed up, it will be almost impossible to tell that he who praises us is a flatterer and liar, because he tells us exactly what pleases us. We easily accept his cunning praise as truth, and the person himself as one who likes us and

is well disposed towards us. But such a deception is very harmful for us, because with such a deception we receive a false understanding of ourselves and become confirmed in this false understanding of ourselves. And with a false understanding of ourselves, our reform, and consequently our salvation, is quite impossible.

3. Do not think that these warnings are unfounded and that any sensible person can immediately see a flatterer and will not be taken in by the deception. In reality, the deception almost always works. Anyone who wants to obtain something useful, beneficial, or pleasant for himself from someone else always catches that person in a net of praise. This net is almost never escaped from, and the captive often with pleasure allows himself to be dragged off and frequently even considers it an honor.

4. Do not think that because the technique of disposing others favorably to oneself by false praise is a bad one, only few people can use it, and that honest people will certainly not use it. A truly honest person indeed will not lower himself to flattery and hypocrisy. But at the same time, beware: toadying is the favorite and universal means everywhere in the world of gaining advantages and favor from others. Millions employ this technique without hesitation, and no one thinks at all that by his flattery he might incur the indignation of the one whom he is flattering. So great and universal is the predominance on earth of self-love, vainglory, and pride. Be on your guard! Be careful!

5. That you may not fall into pride, vainglory, carelessness, or other ruinous delusion in the face either of deserved or, especially, undeserved praise, as unfortunately so often happens:

a) Try to look with distrust on the praise given you, and if the praise is continued for a long time, then it is best to interrupt the conversation politely and turn it to another topic.

b) Remember well that what is worthy of praise in you is not yours, but God's. It was, indeed, something we acquired because we tried to acquire it, but who gave us the disposition, ability, strength, desire, and opportunity to obtain it, if not God? *What hast thou that thou didst not receive? now if thou didst receive it, why dost thou glory, as if thou hadst not received it?* the Holy Apostle Paul tells the man with self-esteem (I Cor. 4:7). So, when you perceive in yourself something worthy of praise, immediately ascribe it not to yourself, but to the Lord God, saying with the Psalmist, *Not unto us, O Lord, not unto us, but unto thy name give glory* (Ps. 113:9).

6. When you perceive in yourself something worthy of praise, and you feel a desire to tell others about it, try immediately to destroy this desire with the thought that you will not receive any benefit from relating it, but only harm. People are very fickle in their opinions: what they praise today, they forget or even condemn tomorrow. And of course, by telling of what is praiseworthy in you, you are making yourself unworthy of praise from God, because you are receiv-

54

ing your reward from people. *Verily I say unto you, they have their reward,* said the Lord of people of this type (Matt. 6:5). Also, try always to remember these important words of the Lord: *Woe unto you, when all men shall speak well of you* (Luke 6:26).

6. How to Conduct Ourselves When People Speak Evil of Us

Our good name is very important for us in life. *A good name is rather to be chosen than great riches,* says the wise Solomon (Prov. 22:1). A good name brings us the respect and trust of others, and we have great need of it in life, because no one wants to have dealings with a dishonest person. Therefore we cannot look indifferently on the opinions of others about us. The dishonest person can expect neither heartfelt compassion nor help from others. And if we are entrusted with any kind of leadership role, it is almost impossible to control subordinates while lacking the respect of others.

So, what should we do when other people, by spreading bad talk about us, deprive us of our good name?

1. First of all, no matter how bad and how injurious the evil talk spread about us may be, we must guard ourselves from anger, verbal abuse, and revenge, but remain as placid as possible in spirit, because we all must be of one spirit with Christ, and Christ, in the face of all the accusations from the Jews, remained in a placid, not in the least bit vengeful, spirit. Christ,

when he was reviled, reviled not again. . . but committed himself to him that judgeth righteously, the holy Apostle Peter says (I Pet. 2:23).

2. When you hear that others are speaking badly of you and ascribing to you vices of various sorts, bad intentions, and so forth, then immediately subject yourself to the strictest examination to see whether the vices they ascribe to you are really there. Perhaps they say you are proud, a liar, an idler, a spendthrift, a drunkard, a sluggard, a debaucher, or whatever else. Examine yourself very closely: don't those vices actually lurk within you, if only to a small degree? Isn't there pride, falsehood, and so on? Other people's eyes often see our conduct much better and more reliably than our own do, because every person has a certain amount of pride, and pride always conceals us from ourselves. Thus, we can rarely see ourselves accurately, and some people, even quite depraved ones, consider themselves faultless. If impartial examination of yourself shows you that others reproach you justly, that one or another vice indeed exists in you, then quickly offer repentance, fervently pray to the Lord God to deliver you from that vice, try zealously to correct yourself of it, and then everywhere show the most sincere friendly disposition and gratitude towards the one who spoke evil of you, regardless of his intentions for doing so, because without his reproach you perhaps would never have seen your vices, would have died without repentance and correction, and would have perished forever.

3. If, after the most attentive, impartial examination of yourself, you find that the vices ascribed to you do not exist, you may legitimately defend yourself and refute the slander leveled at you, but only when finding this necessary not because of your self-love or pride but because of your position in society. But defend yourself calmly, without anger or indignation. Jesus Christ Himself acted thus when they said of Him that He was driving out devils with the help of Beelzebub the prince of devils (Luke 11:15-26).

4. If you see that defending yourself will not do you any good, then:

a) Try to bear the slander leveled at you, no matter how serious, with patience, and console yourself with the thoughts, "God sees my innocence, so what should I grieve about? He Himself cares for me, and, if my vindication will be beneficial for me, then He Himself will vindicate me. He will declare my innocence at the Dread Judgement at least, and all the people and all the Angels of God will vindicate me with Him."

b) Console yourself even more with this thought: "They let forth a great stream of abuse on our Savior when he lived on earth. but He never justified Himself in any court. Some of the abuse was very serious, but He endured everything with equanimity. That is how I should act. *The disciple is not above his master* and *it is enough for the disciple that he be as his master* (Matt. 10:24-25).

c) Double your efforts to conduct yourself as irreproachably as possible in all circumstances of your life.

Endeavor not only to avoid giving others occasion for spiteful talk by any of your words or deeds, but also endeavor to avert any occasion to be even suspected of any vices, and therefore avoid even permissible behavior if it somehow can give cause for slander. Behave this way, and then do not pay attention to the bad talk spread about you. May your conscience and God be the witnesses to your innocence.

d) if the evil talk spread about you does not cease, or even multiplies, then resort to nothing but fervent prayer that the Lord God may have the kindness to enlighten and correct your slanderers. Act this way because Jesus Christ Himself acted this way even with his executioners (Luke 23:34).

7. *How to Conduct Ourselves in Illness*

1. If some illness befalls you, first of all thank God for it, for the Lord God sends every illness for our salvation. Illnesses have always been one of the Lord God's most powerful motivators towards salvation. Without illness, many people would not have come to love God, would never have begun to pay less attention to the temporal, and would never have come to so highly value the eternal, as they do now. Without illness many people would not refrain from vices, as they do now; by means of illness, the Lord God disposes them by force, so to speak, to leave sin and lead a life pleasing to Him. Without illness, many people would become a cause of tears for a countless number of people or a most disastrous plague for

58

human souls; but by means of prolonged or continual illness the All-Good God denies them the opportunity to leave their houses and cause injury to others. By means of illness, He has cut them off from contact with their neighbors; they now are harmless to their neighbors and less harmful to themselves. So, thank the Lord God that He is not depriving you of His grace and is using one of His most powerful tools in the cause of your salvation.

2. While thanking the Lord God for your illness, quickly and as attentively as possible consider how you have especially sinned or continue to sin unrepentantly before Him. But in doing this do not allow pride or anything else to deceive you. It is very probable that you have sinned somehow and are not thinking of repentance. None of us is without sin. *If we say that we have no sin, we deceive ourselves, and the truth is not in us* (I John 1:8). When you find yourself having sinned in something, offer repentance immediately, and make a firm pledge to the Lord not to sin again in that way.

3. But whether you find yourself guilty of something or not, think without fail that the illness that has befallen you may be your last. Very many people die quite unexpectedly from diseases they did not expect to be fatal. Therefore, in good time, without waiting for the disease to take a turn for the worse, try to prepare for death by a proper confession. Do not put off till tomorrow this extremely important matter. For death can descend on you unexpectedly, and the

illness may suddenly worsen to such an extent that confession becomes very difficult or even impossible for you. After confession, receive the Holy Mysteries. This is the best medicine not only for your soul, but also for your body; for with Holy Communion Jesus Christ enters our hearts, and He is the source of all good things.

4. If, in examining your conscience for a good confession, you find that you are in debt to someone, quickly pay him back yourself or give clear instructions that your debt be repaid. If you find that you have someone else's property that you somehow acquired unjustly, return it quickly to its proper owner. If you remember that you have offended someone, or that anyone has offended you, and you harbor hostility, then make up with that person quickly and sincerely. Do not forget the fearful words of the Lord, *When thou goest with thine adversary to the magistrate, as thou art in the way, give diligence that thou mayest be delivered from him; lest he hale thee to the judge, and the judge deliver thee to the officer, and the officer cast thee into prison.* For, *thou shalt not depart thence, till thou hast paid the very last mite* (Luke 12:58-59).

5. When the condition of your soul in relation to eternity is secure in this way , turn your attention to its temporal condition. To wit, try quickly to make legal provisions regarding your property. Do not put it off for long, lest you have to spend the precious last minutes of your life, which you should use only for the soul, on temporal matters, and lest, in mak-

ing your will, you commit some kind of injustice. Do not forget that carelessness in a legal will concerning property very often causes the greatest confusion and frequently hostility among the heirs that lasts their entire lives, and sometimes even after their deaths. Do not be responsible for other people's sins; make a proper will in good time.

6. While doing or after doing this, if you have the opportunity, call a physician and take the medicines that he prescribes. We should not avoid the physician, for *the Lord hath created him* says the wise one (Ecclesiasticus 38:12). But by no means should we think that only the doctor or medicines can do away with your illness. Not the doctor and not medicines, but only the Lord God grants healing. Therefore, at every visit to the doctor, put your hope only on the Lord God, because the Lord God enlightens the doctor and it is He Who gives healing power to the doctor's medicine. *The Lord . . . maketh alive* (I Kings. 2:6).

7. Do not spend your time of illness in idle conversations, nor in excessive care for your recovery, but try to use this time for the benefit of your soul: pray, read a spiritual book, especially one in which the sufferings of the Lord are described, or nourish yourself with pious conversations. If you do not have the strength to engage in long prayers, then raise up your heart to God in short sighs of prayer. For example, "Lord, deprive me not of your mercy!" Or, "Lord, grant that this illness will be for the cleansing of my sins" and so on. Besides this, make the sign of the cross on

yourself and kiss the icons of the Savior, the Mother of God, and the saints often.

8. During your illness, never pray importunately for recovery; it is better to give yourself over to God's will, because only the Lord God truly knows what is best for your salvation: health or illness, weak or robust health, uninterrupted or changeable health, a mild illness or a serious one, a short or prolonged one, or even one persisting until death. If health is ruinous for our souls, how can we pray immoderately to God for it? It would be better never to be healthy. If illness is salvific for us, how can we ask unreservedly for deliverance from it? It would be better to remain ill and to endure the most severe illness until death itself.

9. If your illness lasts a very long time, do not lapse, as many foolish people do, into impatience, especially into grumbling and bad temper at the seriousness and length of the illness, at the doctor, at the medicine, at the bad weather, at those who are serving you, and so on. You will never relieve your illness, not to mention eliminate it, by impatience, grumbling, and bad temper. An impatient and especially a grumbling disposition of soul may, on the one hand, only aggravate the illness and prolong it or even make it incurable, and on the other hand, turn off others' sympathy for you, for who finds it pleasant to wait on a sick person when he is irritable and foul-tempered towards those serving him? On the contrary, be as patient as possible and pray thus: "O Lord, I have sinned much and am worthy of eternal torment, but

in Your boundless love, You do not want me to suffer eternally but have subjected me to a temporal punishment, so that I may come to myself, repent, and reform. How great is Thy mercy. Multiply my patience; grant me such grace that I may endure my illness in good spirits and with love for Thee. It is better for me to wish that my illness may get worse, rather than that it cease, and I began again to sin and be subjected to eternal torments. Let my illness continue and get worse if it pleases You, only deliver me from eternal torments."

10. When you feel that the illness is ebbing, and you are beginning to get well, then pray to the Lord God that, after the return of your health, He will be pleased to keep you from every sin and will give you a firm memory of those sensations and thoughts that you had during your illness, for very many sick people after the return of their health forget the sensations that they had during their illness. Pray to the Lord God that it would be better for Him to keep you ill or even to let you die, rather than for you to return to a sinful life after your recovery.

11. On the other hand, if you feel that your illness is worsening and is beginning to exhaust your bodily strength, receive the Mystery of Holy Unction. The Lord God greatly heals the body by it, and if He is not pleased to heal your body, He will certainly heal your soul. *The Lord shall raise him [the sick man] up; and if he have committed sins, they shall be forgiven him*, says the holy Apostle (James 5:15).

12. After doing this, entrust yourself completely to the will of God and do not wish for anything other than that the Lord God do with you whatever is pleasing to Him. This is the best attitude for every person, whatever his condition. Because whoever entrusts himself to the Lord God is God's, and such a one can never perish.

8. How to Protect Ourselves from the Harmful Effect of Bad Example

In the world, we are never without bad example, and bad example is highly contagious: It sometimes produces a sinful contagion in people even after the causes of that contagion are long dead. And this sinful contagion is set in motion not only by some particularly depraved behavior of people, but often only by their glance or their joking and laughter, while they themselves for the most part do not notice or realize it. How can we protect ourselves from contagion by such harmful effects? Here are some ways.

1. Remove yourself in every way possible from all circumstances in which you are inescapably forced to see and hear a lot of bad things. There is company in which bad conversations are a usual or even a favorite way to pass the time. There are amusements in which the tendency to sensual pleasure finds the most plentiful nourishment. Those fond of frequenting such settings can easily throw their hearts into confusion and become entangled in the web of seduction. Therefore, do not give in to any persuasive invitations to them;

do not allow yourself even to tell yourself how commonplace the amusement is in these places, and how bad example will produce nothing bad in your heart. Whatever has not been seen, heard, and so on, will not come into your mind.

2. When you encounter bad examples unexpectedly or must encounter them by necessity, then try to make the evil that you see create in you a revulsion to it, which it naturally creates and should create in all of us. Besides this, turn immediately to the Lord God with the heartfelt prayer: "All-merciful God! Preserve me that I may never do such evil and that even the memory of it may be obliterated from my memory." Whoever acts thus has in his hand a strong shield against the harmful effect of bad example.

3. To preserve yourself from the harmful effect of bad example, try to provide yourself ahead of time with good rules and information about examples of true virtue. When the Jews were taken captive by the Babylonians, and many of them were taken off to Babylon, the Prophet Jeremias feared nothing for the captives in the idol-worshipping capital as much as their seduction into idol worship. He therefore wrote to them: "Now shall ye see in Babylon gods of silver, and of gold, and of wood . . . . Beware therefore that ye in no wise be like to strangers . . . when ye see the multitude . . . worshipping them. But say ye [to the Lord God] in your hearts, O Lord, we must worship Thee" (Baruch 6: 4-6). This is how we should act as well. When we see that many people are idolized,

but the Only-Begotten Son of the eternal Father is not deemed worthy even of attention; when we hear that the foolish and disastrous opinions of the spirit of the time are glorified as perfect wisdom, but coolness or even disdain are shown to the teachings of the Christian faith; when we see that the most salvific injunctions for the salvation of immortal souls are passed off as a human matter and that it is alleged that only gullibility can hold to such injunctions; then we must immediately say in our hearts, as the holy apostles said: *Jesus Christ is Lord of lords, and King of kings* (Rev. 17:14); *at His name every knee should bow, of things in heaven, and things in earth, and things under the earth* (Philip. 2:10); *there is none other . . . whereby we must be saved* (Acts 4:12). *He that believeth not the Son shall not see life* (John 3:36), *but he that believeth not shall be damned* (Mark 16:16). When we see that many people avidly seek their happiness in sensual pursuits, in sensual pleasures, in comfort, and in luxury and pass this off as wisdom; when we see that the children of the world use every falsehood and every deception to construct their earthly happiness; when we hear that they defend hatred, vindictiveness, and other passions, but consider refusal to satisfy sensual desires to be foolishness; then we must resolutely say in our hearts, as the holy apostles taught: "We are Christians; we must *fulfill the law of Christ* (Gal. 6:2)", and the law of Christ requires that we *have crucified the flesh with the affections and lusts* (Gal. 5:24), put away lying and speak the truth (Eph. 4:25), and have yielded vengeance to the Lord God. For *vengeance is mine; I will repay, saith the Lord* (Rom. 12:19).

4. In all occurrences of bad example, look immediately to Jesus Christ, Who has the full right to demand that we follow His example, and then look to the millions of people who had previously been more or less sinners like us, but then became holy in Christ and worthy of imitation by their imitation of His life. Imitate not the example of coldness towards God, which is everywhere apparent in the world, but rather the example of the zeal of Jesus Christ and the saints, about which Christian history relates so much that is edifying. Imitate not the example of pagan life, which is so often apparent in the world, but the example of good behavior, modesty, sense of shame, temperance, and decency by which were distinguished the saints, or the true Christians, who constantly lived not by the rules of the world, but by the teachings of the Lord Jesus Christ.

HOW SHOULD WE CONDUCT OURSELVES IN OUR DAILY WORK?

Our daily work, depending on our position and the profession in which we live, is quite diverse. There is manual work, that is, all manner of trades, agriculture, and so forth. There is intellectual work, such as reflection and thought, administration, justice, management, education, and so forth. There is important and unimportant work, difficult and easy, extraordinary and conventional, work for yourself, your family, for society, etc.

We must acknowledge all such everyday work that is not opposed to moral law and that we must do according to our position, as God's work, as work entrusted to us by the Lord God Himself. We must acknowledge our daily work as such because the Lord God established various sanctioned positions and professions in human society, and it was the Lord God, and not we, Who put us or allows us to be in the positions or professions in which we find ourselves in life. Without God's will or God's forbearance nothing takes place on earth. *God is the King of all the earth* (Ps. 46:8). Therefore, the holy Apostle Paul instructed slaves, who were working not for themselves, but for their masters, that they actually worked not for their masters, but for the Lord Himself. *Servants,* he wrote in his Epistle to the Colossians, *obey in all things your masters, except, of course, for sin, and whatsoever ye do, do it heartily, as to the Lord, and not unto men* (Col. 3:22, 23). And so:

1. Whatever work you have to do in accordance with your position and profession, whether it is to hold the reins of some governmental organ, to judge someone, to teach someone, to write something, to engage in some kind of art or handiwork, to plow the fields, to sow grain, to reap or to thresh, to mow and gather hay, and so on, do all of this, for whomever you do it, whether for yourself and your family, or as a duty to others, do all this as if for the Lord God Himself, that is, do it because the Lord God demands it from you, and because that work is God's work—do

it and say in your soul to God: "O Lord, You assigned me this work: I am doing it in obedience to You and to please you." Or: "O Lord, bless my labor. It was not without Your will that I found myself in the position in which I live, and the work that I do or should do is the work demanded by my position. You assigned it to me, so bless me and help me."

Whoever does his daily work with such a disposition of spirit, no matter what it is and for whom he does it, works actually for the Lord God, and therefore will receive the reward from the Lord God Himself, as the holy apostle attests to slaves, *when instructing them whatsoever ye do for your masters in the flesh, do it heartily, as to the Lord, and not unto men, he says, knowing that of the Lord ye shall receive the reward of the inheritance: for ye serve the Lord Christ* (Col. 3:23, 24). But whoever labors without this disposition of soul, labors as all worldly people and pagans do, that is, he labors not for the Lord Jesus Christ, not out of love for the Lord God, not to the glory of God, but labors either only for himself, for some temporary need or gain: for his own sustenance, to pay zemstvo obligations, to gain wealth, prosperity, and pleasure in life, to obtain honors, glory, high esteem, to satisfy his inquisitiveness, and so on, or he labors temporarily for other people. He does not even think of the Lord God. But the work of whoever works like this is very pitiful, because he must await a reward only from himself, or from other people, and not from the Lord God. But the reward from other people, whatever it consists of, can be and always is only earthly, temporary, and therefore of little importance; what kind of a reward is one you get from yourself? Work for the Lord God, and expect your reward principally from Him. Only He is the true recompenser (Rom. 12:19; Heb. 1:6).

2. In doing all your work for the Lord God Himself, always do them as God's work should be done, that is, do all your work from the soul, that is to say, gladly, with great pleasure, and—especially—without grumbling. How can one do any kind of work for the Lord God unwillingly, grudgingly, and even more, with grumbling? Any grateful person does everything with pleasure even for his low-ranking earthly boss; how can we do something unwillingly or grudgingly for our greatest, incessant benefactor, for the Lord God?

3. Do every task required by your position and profession diligently and correctly; do not in any case permit unwarranted slowness and carelessness. Do everything as well as you possibly can, with a clear conscience. Because work done with any kind of culpable slowness, just as work done incorrectly, carelessly, or at least not as quickly and as well as you can, is done, not to speak of anything else, deceitfully, and the holy prophet says, *cursed be he that doeth the work of the Lord deceitfully* (Jer. 48:10). My friends, remember these terrible words and be careful!

4. If your work goes successfully, do not take pride in this, and in particular do not ascribe the success

71

in your work to your own powers. *Never say in your heart my power and the might of mine hand hath gotten me this wealth* (Deut. 8:17). Rather always remember well that the Lord gave you that power (Deut. 8:18). For without me ye can do nothing, He said to His disciples (John 15:5). Remember well these words of the Lord. They are a great bulwark against pride and arrogance to which all of us are so very inclined and which is so clearly ruinous for all of us.

5. If the work that you must do is difficult and demands particular effort, or unpleasant and demeaning and demands particular patience, or is hindered, slowed, or upset by ill-intentioned people or by unfortunate circumstances, and leads you to despondency, or is little respected and even despised, do not be fainthearted, do not be lazy, and do not give in to any hostile feelings; do not give in to anger, impatience, vexation, grumbling, and so on. Will your work go better and will it be finished faster if you are, for example, lazy, grumble, are vexed or angry, use bad language? No, it will always go worse and more slowly, or may not even get done at all. My friend, it is bad to behave this way. Do not behave this way; only pagans behave like this, because they do not have faith in God's rule over the world. But we are Christians. We know that our work in our position in life is the work of God.

6. In order to help in keeping your soul in a holy disposition during hard, prolonged, or unpleasant work and to protect it from any disposition that

is not God-pleasing, it is very good to enliven and strengthen yourself with the following thoughts

a) "The work, which seems to me to be so difficult and unpleasant, is undoubtedly very salvific for my soul. God does nothing without the most saving intentions for us. He very much wants to save all people. Therefore, of course, He desires the same for me. Without His action and foresight, I would have been lost long ago. Having assigned me the work at hand, He undoubtedly wishes to deliver me from grievous sins or from serious temptations, errors of great consequence, or other dangers. I shall do my work diligently and wholeheartedly." Or:

b) "The work that I am doing is, perhaps, the last in my life, and after this work God will immediately demand an account from me of all my deeds at His Judgment in eternity. How can I not work diligently and wholeheartedly?" Or:

c) "These labors, which are such a burden to me and are so unaccustomed and vexing for me, will not last forever. They will end with my earthly life. And is earthly life long, even if it lasts a hundred years? All of eternity is the reward for life on earth, if it is spent in obedience to the Lord God. How can I not work diligently and wholeheartedly?"

If you think such thoughts, your heavy, difficult, or unpleasant work will never serve as a cause for sin, but will always be a means for purification from sin and for eternal blessedness. Because, in thinking this, you will of course never avoid your work, no matter how difficult or unpleasant it may seem, but will pray in your heart to the Lord God, that He help you to begin, continue, and finish it equably, and you will indeed do so. And meanwhile, you will be delivered perhaps from some very serious sins and from the perdition of your soul. For the Lord God, after such a prayer, as holy toilers have already found out a thousand times by experience, often eased the difficulty and unpleasantness of various hard daily labors to the point where they did them and finished them without difficulty and unpleasantness, and even sometimes very easily and with pleasure. But if this never happens to us, we must remember well that every diligent work and every diligent worker will be indeed rewarded appropriately, not in the present life, but in the the future one. Our reward is not here, but in the future life. It is precisely there, as the holy apostle attests, [the Lord] *will render to every man according to his deeds* (Rom. 2:6). Let us be patient! Are not all our temporary burdens and difficulties worth eternal happiness?

7. If the work that you are doing is prolonged, unpleasant, hard, and is someone else's as well, then to keep your soul in a holy and God-pleasing disposition and to protect yourself from any foolish disposition of soul, support yourself while you work with edifying singing, as long as it is not ruled out by the work itself or the place and time. Edifying singing greatly cheers, softens, and calms the soul. If, as is well known, even unedifying, foolish singing during work

greatly cheers a person as he works, so much more will edifying singing. If you see that your singing arouses great indignation against you among others, and thus not only cuts off their love for you, but also enflames malice, then stop singing, and pray silently. Otherwise, do not pay attention to others and continue to sing as you were singing. Most likely, your always steady demeanor will finally teach those around you, or, at least, make them leave you in peace.

8. For the same reason, during physical labor, if this labor is mechanical, reflect about truths that you previously heard in a sermon or read in an edifying book.

9. But especially occupy yourself for this purpose in reflection on the work that you do, whether it is demanded by your position or by your duty.

Are you a joiner? During your work, you may easily nourish yourself with very saving truths. While making a coffin, you can think, "Such is a person's last home. In time, all of us will take up residence in such a home. Rich and poor will settle in it. The huge house in which the rich man lives at present will not exempt him from this home. The poor man will not feel embarrassed in this home because it is not expensively decorated, like the home of the rich man." And in thinking these thoughts, you will finally say: "All things are vanity. All things will pass away. In time we shall all lie in a coffin. Even I shall lie in one."

While making a cross for a grave, you can say to yourself: "On a cross like this, the Lord Jesus Christ poured out His precious blood. What an enormous good deed He did for us. Do I thank Him and bear the cross that He commanded us to bear in life? How ungrateful I am towards Him. All-Merciful Lord, grant me clear vision and strength, that I may always and everywhere clearly see my cross and bear it with a good nature."

Making a door, you can readily remember that the Lord said of Himself, *I am the door: by me if any man enter in, he shall be saved* (John 10:9), and having recalled this, you will think that as into every house we enter only by the door, so also we may only enter the heavenly kingdom through Jesus Christ and His merits. Without the Lord Jesus Christ, there is no entry for us into the Kingdom of Heaven. *Neither is there salvation in any other, except the Lord Jesus Christ* (Acts 4:12). Such thoughts will form in your soul the most profound gratitude to the Lord and will greatly ease your labor.

Are you a locksmith? While doing your work you can easily have very soul-saving thoughts. While making a lock, you can think that because of mankind's sins, heaven was locked shut for all of us and that if the Son of God had not had the loving kindness to unlock it by His sufferings and death, they would even now remain locked, so that no strong, famous, renowned person could unlock them neither for himself nor for other people, and all of us would have to live outside the kingdom of God. But life outside the Kingdom of God is terrible. Everyone who does not enter the Kingdom of God will live for eternity, as the holy Apostle John states, *in the lake which burneth with fire and brimstone* (Rev. 21:8).

Are you a cook? It is quite appropriate for you to reason just as did one of the ancient cooks in a monastic habitation. "The work entrusted to me," he told everyone, "is very soul-saving for me. I suffer pain when I move my hand only somewhat close to the fire, and I immediately try to pull it away. And whenever I have to pick up from the floor a burning coal that has fallen out of the oven and throw it back in, then it hurts very much. When this happens, I think: what will happen when I die without cleansing my sins by repentance and faith in the purifying death of Christ? How harsh will my suffering be when I am thrown into the blazing fire and am kept there without chance of escape? Centuries, ages will go by, but even then I shall have nothing to say about my torments, except that they have begun, because there will be no end to my torments. This is what I think about, and I strictly avoid any sin." My friend, you should reason this way too. Such thoughts will powerfully preserve you from sin and will bind you with faith to God, the Savior of the world, and, if you have a living faith, will also form in you a living faith in Him.

Are you a tailor? While making clothing for others, you can think: "All of these clothes are quite durable and in the end will have no significance. The only things that are durable and significant are the wedding garments that the Lord spoke about in the parable about the wedding of His son." In addition, you can easily think: "Do I have this vitally important wedding garment?" The Lord commanded that the man who appeared at the wedding without a wedding garment be bound and thrown *into outer darkness, where there is weeping and gnashing of teeth* (Matt. 22:13). Therefore, I very much need to obtain this wedding garment. Only those clothed in this garment will be admitted to the wedding, that is, into the eternal and most blessed kingdom of the Son of God. No other garment, no matter how expensive and skillfully sewn, is suitable (Rev. 19:14)." So, consider, my friend. Frequent reflection on the wedding garment may easily dispose you to diligently seek the wedding garment by a firm faith in the Savior of the world. The Lord, without doubt, will grant it to you, and you will enter into His eternal joy (Matt. 25:23).

Are you a shoemaker? You may very appropriately think about the humility that St. John the Baptist showed when others, marveling at his teaching and his very strict way of life, would ask him, "Are you the Christ?" John did not only not usurp the name of Christ, but even said that he was not worthy even to unloose the latchet of Christ's shoes (John 1:27), That is, not worthy even to take Christ's shoes off. Thinking like this, you can very easily acquire the zeal to keep humble and distance yourself from pride, which everyone knows is characteristic only of the devil and of people who follow his suggestions.

Are you a carpenter? Finishing wood and joining one piece with another so that a well-made house results, you can easily think: "This is also how I must finish my coarse heart so that it becomes God's house, for all of us must become worthy habitations of God, because every single one of us prays each morning to the Lord God as directed by the Holy Church "come and abide in us."

A blacksmith may also nourish his soul with saving truths. Looking at the hammer he is using and the nails he has made, he can at once very easily recollect that our Lord Jesus Christ was nailed to the cross with a similar hammer and with nails such as those. What terrible pain He felt from the nails! And He bore this terrible pain out of love for me, in order for my sins to be forgiven and so that I would not burn in the fire of Hell, similar to how I fire up iron in the forge so that it will be suitable for making horseshoes. What unspeakable kindness! Such an unspeakable kindness that was shown to us precisely out of love for us should release all of our hearts from everything and make them adhere with all their might to love only for the Lord Jesus Christ with His beginningless and all-good Father and the Holy Spirit.

Stonemasons during their work can easily think that in the same way they finish stone, they should work on themselves in order to make themselves into a temple of God, pure and holy. *For the temple of God is holy* (I Cor. 3:17). And each of us must become the temple of God. *Know ye not that ye are the temple of*

79

God, and that the Spirit of God dwelleth in you? says the holy Apostle Paul to the believers of Corinth (I Cor. 3:16).

A clock maker may very easily and savingly bring to mind that even with the help of clocks no one *know[s] neither the day nor the hour wherein the Son of man cometh* (Matt. 25:13), and that everyone must constantly prepare for His coming (Matt. 24:44), not looking at any clocks, and that otherwise all of us, even with the very best clocks, will, like the foolish virgins, remain outside His bridal chamber (Matt. 25:10). We should not spend a single minute in such a way that will not be a preparation for the coming of the Lord, but every moment await His appearance, especially because the Lord has said, *be ye. . .ready: for in such an hour as ye think not the Son of man cometh* (Matt. 24:44).

A glazier undoubtedly often notices that glass immediately loses its luster when even a light human breath touches it, and therefore he may easily think that a person's conscience loses its luster exactly in the same way, when even a light breath of some evil passion touches it, and that therefore every one of us must hurry and try to destroy in himself every passion, no matter how pleasurable it may be for us, and no matter how accustomed we are to it.

A bookbinder, constantly turning over various books in his hands, may very easily bring to mind those books that will be opened at the Dread Judgment and in which all our actions and feelings are accurately recorded (Rev. 20:12). Calling to mind these books, he will in every way possible take care to efface from them all his bad actions and feelings, using faith in the crucified Lord and repentance, and at the same time will strive earnestly for his name to be written in the book of life (Rev. 20:15).

A baker may very easily call to mind the Lord's exceedingly important words: I am that bread of life. *[I]f any man eat of this bread, he shall live for ever: and the bread that I will give is my flesh, which I will give for the life of the world* (John 6:48, 51). And with such a remembrance of these words of the Lord each of us should ask ourselves the questions: do I receive the Lord's Body and Blood? Do I receive them often? If I do receive them, do I receive them worthily? And if I do not receive them, then why not? As communion is very salvific for us, because the Lord said, *whoso eateth my flesh, and drinketh my blood, hath eternal life* (John 6:54), so not receiving communion is very hurtful to us, because the Lord said, *except ye eat the flesh of the Son of man, and drink his blood, ye have no life in you* (John 6:53), that is, you are not living life in God, you do not live piously, and consequently, you live impiously. So, I must firmly remember these words of the Lord and try to fulfill them, in no way following the manifestly ruinous practice of those people who do not receive the Body and Blood of Christ. Here is more on how every baker may easily bring to mind the Lord's words, *man shall not live by bread alone, but by every word that proceedeth out of the mouth of God*

(Matt. 4:4), and ask himself, "Do I read, or listen to the Word of God? If I read it, do I read it according to the guidance of the Holy Church? And if I do not read or listen to it, then why not? The Word of God contains the rules according to which we must conduct our lives, that they may be pleasing to God, and that we may finally be found worthy to be in the Kingdom of God."

It is very good for the farmer to recollect the Lord's beautiful parable about the seed (Matt. 13:4-9) and to take great care, lest he remain rocky and infertile ground, but to strive indefatigably to form himself into fertile ground.

The gardener may reflect with great edification on the Lord's saying *every tree that bringeth not forth good fruit is hewn down, and cast into the fire* (Matt. 7:19) and try to make himself a tree that bears good fruit. It is salvific also for him to reflect on the barren fig tree (Matt. 21:19-20) and to try to become fruitful. It is also very edifying for the gardener, noticing the delicacy, beauty, and splendor of various flowers that grow in his garden, to think that the saints blossom in God's great garden even more beautifully and to try to become a saint himself in order to occupy, like them, some place in God's great garden and not to find himself outside it, not to be thrown into the fire together with the weeds.

It is very salvific for a candle maker to think that the true light that enlightens every man is the Lord Jesus Christ alone (John 8:12; 1:9), that all of us should as much as possible walk in this light, that is, by the teaching of the Holy Gospel (John 12:35) and be sons of the light (John 12:36), lest we in the end fall into the terrible outer darkness (John 12:35). *I am the light of the world*, said the Lord, *he that followeth me shall not walk in darkness, but shall have the light of life* (John 8:12).

A beekeeper may very easily call to mind the highly soul-saving saying of the holy King David, *how sweet to my palate are Thy sayings! more sweet than honey to my mouth* (Ps. 118:103). And this recollection may arouse the thought in any beekeeper, "How very pleasant was God's Word to the saints." And such a thought might readily dispose him to listen to the word of God more fervently and attentively. *For the word of God is quick, and powerful* (Heb. 4:12). It will not remain without a saving influence on the mind and heart of whoever hears or reads it.

These and similar reflections during our physical labors direct our souls very powerfully to the good and, regardless of the labor, strengthen the body itself.

10. To keep the soul in a holy disposition during prolonged labor, and in particular to keep yourself from boredom, from grumbling, from vexation, and from impatience, it is again very helpful during work to raise your heart to the Lord God frequently in short prayerful petitions that fit the state and disposition of your heart. For example, the following petitions are very helpful: "How boundlessly the Lord God loves us"; "How much He does for us"; "How

much He gives us"; "O God, how grateful we should be towards Thee"; "O Lord, bless me, purify me, enlighten me, and sanctify me"; "Only Thou, O Lord, lovest us so much; how can we not love Thee with all our hearts. Whom shall we love with all our hearts, if not Thee?" "Ah! if only all people knew how good thou art, O Lord." "Oh, if only such and such a bad habit were rooted out of me." "Oh, if only I knew my heart well." "Oh, if only I could see more clearly the insignificance of this world." "Oh, if only I could love Thee, O Lord, with my whole heart." "Ah, Lord, some day I will serve Thee with all my soul." "Ah, Lord, if only I constantly remembered You and thought about You." "Oh, my God, without You, what is the whole world to me? What benefit or joy can it give me?" "Lord, You are my refuge, You are my comfort, You are my hope, You are my tranquillity, You are my light, You are my glory, You are my joy, You are my blessedness, and everything else." "Lord, when will this world cease to trouble me with various temptations?" "Lord, when will the end come to all hindrances to salvation and mood changes?" "Lord, when will I see you?" "Lord, when will I be with You?" "Lord, when will I be eternally praising you together with all the saints?"

The more often you use such petitions the better, because the more often you repeat them, the more easily they turn into a habit. And these and other such petitions used during work are quite invaluable. These petitions, continuously joining the soul with God, constantly enliven it, drive every evil away from it, strengthen it in goodness, and quite beneficially strengthen the physical powers.

11. Whoever does his daily work in this way is, while toiling to maintain his physical life, working at the same time just as much or even more for the salvation of his soul. He works as he ought to work, for the glory of God. And the holy apostle commands us to do all to the glory of God (I Cor. 10:31).

Note. Of course, it stands to reason that first of all we must do the most important, urgent tasks, that we must start tasks having considered beforehand how to do them best, and that we should never do work that is incompatible with the law of God.

HOW SHOULD WE CONDUCT
OURSELVES DURING MEALS?

Never begin lunch or dinner, or finish them, without fervent prayer to the Lord God as, unfortunately, very many Christians of our time do. One cannot but marvel at how these Christians have reached such a condition of soul that they can both start a meal and finish it without a fervent prayer to the Lord God. For it is precisely the Lord God Who supplies us with all our food. Granted, we ourselves also worked to obtain our food, but what would all our work amount to if the Lord God did not give us His blessing—if, for example, He did not bestow the proper warmth, moisture, wind and sun on the fields and gardens that we have cultivated and sown? Absolutely nothing, as, of course, everyone knows. Besides, it is precisely the Lord God Who furnishes our food with nourishing properties, and our bodies with an ability to use these nourishing properties for our bodily health. What would happen to us if the Lord God had not given nutritional quality to our food? Then no matter how much of even the most nutritious food we consumed, we would not gain bodily strength, and therefore would be able neither to carry out our daily bodily functions nor to continue life itself. Then none of us would remain alive. On the other hand, what would happen to us if the Lord God took away from our stomachs the power of digestion, if only for two weeks? Then even the most nourishing food would not nourish us, but exhaust us and lead us into illness or deprive us of life itself. For experience bears witness that sometimes the healthiest food can be harmful.

Our meals should always be moderate. All the saints, who customarily watched strictly after themselves, say with one voice: 1) that very little is needed for satisfaction of our bodies; 2) that our bellies by themselves almost never know moderation; 3) that our bellies sometimes demand food even when they have had more than enough, and 4) that therefore to maintain moderation it is best to cease consumption of food when the urge to eat has still not completely subsided. St. John Chrysostom gave an excellent rule for observing necessary moderation in food: "Eat just enough to alleviate your hunger." Another holy teacher said "You should not eat whatever you want , but eat what you have, and in a way that after eating and drinking, you still feel an urge for food."

Speaking of food, the saints very forcefully observed that lay people should consume very little, and that for monks, widowers, and widows it is best to completely avoid foods that are filling, stimulating, indigestible, good-tasting, or sweet. Good-tasting or sweet foods because we very easily overindulge in such, and nutritious, stimulating, or indigestible foods because these in particular stir up the bad tendencies of our flesh, and because while using them it is almost impossible to restrain and destroy these tendencies.

Food is, however, necessary for the body. We should not refuse the body necessary food. On the one hand, we need to satisfy the natural demand of nature that we support our health and bodily powers, which are necessary for satisfaction of various needs of body and soul. On the other hand, while lacking food necessary for the body, we may stir up against ourselves an enemy, who perhaps otherwise would not even think of being our enemy.

At meals, especially dinner, never consume food immoderately or to excess. Our food is a gift from God, and all gifts of God, being divine, should be received reverently, decorously, with the fear of God, and consumed only for the purpose for which they are given. Our food is given to us for not for satiety, but for satisfaction.

Satiety is extremely harmful for our body, because stomach disorder, corruption of the blood, various diseases of the body, and premature death are in great part a result of excess or intemperance. Doctors, experience, and the Spirit of God attest to this. *For excess of meats bringeth sickness. . . by surfeiting have many perished, says the Wise One* (Ecclus 37:33,34).

Satiety is extremely harmful for the soul Whoever overindulges in food or drink is incapable of spiritual exercises and can neither pray nor reflect on anything divine, because excess in food draws a person into laziness, sleepiness, idleness, idle talk, ludicrous behavior, and a great multitude of impure thoughts and desires. And for inflammation of anger and love of pleasure it often plays the same role as oil poured onto fire. In general, whoever overeats does not have the true God, but his own flesh and its desires. Therefore, whoever overeats is capable of violating even the holiest obligations and is prepared to commit the most vile acts. Whoever has observed himself and those close to him to any extent needs no proof in this regard.

During lunch and dinner never say anything sinful. Because to insult God at the same time as you are eating His gifts, when it is especially necessary to feel and show gratitude to God, is the vilest ingratitude. But unfortunately, during lunch and dinner many carry on the most impious conversations: they defame, condemn, mock each other, especially absent neighbors, tell suggestive jokes, give themselves up to ludicrous behavior, speak disrespectfully of the faith, of various sacred subjects relating to the faith, and so on. Such conduct over lunch and dinner is extreme ingratitude to the Lord God. Guard against it in every way possible.

During lunch and dinner one should say or listen to something edifying: from sacred history, from the lives of the saints, from natural history revealing God's wisdom and goodness, from spiritual teachings, and so on. Because at the table a person becomes somewhat sluggish and sleepy from food, true Christians try during meals principally to remember death and the dread judgement more vividly in order to keep themselves in a God-pleasing spirit, inaccessible to any depravity. Because it often happens that poorly cooked food may be served, the saints, to keep themselves in such a case from offending, usually imagined immediately that all of us, by our sins and by our constant insult to God, are unworthy not only of what is now being offered, but even of pigs' swill. And then they consumed a certain amount of the food offered as if it had been cooked properly.

Whoever consumes his lunch and dinner thus, that is, moderately and with gratitude to the Lord God, is acting as duty demands, in a righteous and God-pleasing manner. Perhaps in his home there will not be abundance, but at the same time there will never be complete poverty. The Holy Prophet David says, *I have been young, and now am old; yet have I not seen the righteous forsaken, nor his seed begging bread.* On the contrary, the righteous man often finds himself even in *such a position that He is ever merciful, and lendeth* (Ps. 37:25,26), that is, every day he sustains the poor and provides them with something.

And so, whoever does not have his daily bread should examine himself attentively and dispassionately to determine whether he prays for his daily bread to the Lord God before his lunch and dinner and whether he labors for his daily bread. Whoever either does not pray to the Lord God or does not labor should not be surprised if he does not have his daily bread: he will reap what he has sown. *If any would not work, neither should he eat,* the Apostle Paul says (II Thess. 3:10).

HOW SHOULD WE CONDUCT OURSELVES DURING REST AFTER LUNCH?

After lunch, we certainly need to rest, because neither our bodily nor our mental powers can be under constant stress: both need rest. But rest must always be used like a medicine. The frequent, and especially the continual, use of medicine is harmful for the body; frequent idleness is harmful for the soul. The enemy of our salvation uses nothing so confidently for our perdition as our inactivity, our idleness. What a multitude of foolish thoughts come to the minds of idle people! *Idleness teacheth much evil,* says the Wise One (Eccles. 33:28 in Slavonic; Eccles. 30:27 in Bagster's). In this regard, Saint Barsonuphius the Great said: "Bodily rest is loathsome in the sight of the Lord."

Therefore, one should never spend much time at rest. Having rested a little, each of us should think, "What rest is there in the present world? The Holy Spirit says, that they may rest from their labours (not concerning us), who have our health and life, but about the dead which die in the Lord (Rev. 14:13). For us, real rest will be in the future life." Blessedness in heaven is appointed for and given to us not for our rest or for idleness, but for our labors. *Every man shall receive his own reward according to his own labour, says the holy apostle* (I Cor. 3:8). Very foolish was that person who in the present life said to himself, *take thine ease* (Luke 12:19). After saying this, he quite naturally was compelled by his passions to say, *eat, drink, and be merry* (Luke 12:19). In the future life the Lord will grant neither a share in His blessedness nor the slightest comfort to people of this type, but will say, as Abraham said to the foolish rich man: *remember that thou in thy lifetime receivedst thy good things* (Luke 16:25). Everyone rising from a meal should think of this and, after having rested a little, get back to work.

Never use time for rest, as do many foolish people, on amusements or on any dissolute or useless games, for example, card-playing, pitch-and-toss, and so forth. Concerning amusements St. Basil the Great says, "Amusement is the mother of sin. Amusement is the food of the eternal worm," among other things. Games generally inculcate idleness, laziness, and many other vices. While playing games people very often and almost inescapably wish evil for others, lie, deceive, become annoyed, irritated or angry, taunt each other with venomous words, swear without need, often become involved in irreconcilable hostility, pointlessly squander their resources, and, in any case, trifle away their precious time.

To prevent any ungodly thoughts from entering your head or ungodly desires from entering your heart during necessary rest, try to nourish yourself, depending on the condition of your soul, with various spiritual thoughts, and especially with appeals of the heart to the Lord God; for example, "O Lord, how great is Thy wisdom and goodness! Each day Thou givest nourishment to a countless multitude of living creations on the earth—people, birds, livestock, beasts, insects, and all of them are satisfied and none dies from hunger." Or: "How happy everyone on earth would be if all of its envy, miserliness, pride, and ill-will were wiped out." Or: "All-merciful God, do not deprive me in heaven of the rest that Thy beloved enjoy, a rest that truly gives relief from all tiring labors and to which there will be no end," and so on.

Such reflections and appeals will far more quickly renew our bodily powers than all other methods of renewal, and they greatly strengthen the soul in good deeds.

HOW SHOULD WE CONDUCT OURSELVES IN THE EVENING?

In the evening, when your daily business should be finished, by no means give yourself over to rest, no matter how much the activities of the day have tired you. It is unbecoming for a Christian to act ungrateful this way. When you have finished your business, lift up your thoughts to the Lord God and sincerely thank Him for all the good things that you have received from Him in the day that is coming to a close, that is, for having stayed alive, for your spiritual and bodily strength, for your health, for food, for drink, for all soul-saving thoughts, for all holy desires, for earthly and heavenly light, for help and protection--in short, for every good thing.

When you sit down to dinner, always start and finish it with a prayer, as you do at lunch.

After dinner, just as in the morning after breakfast, occupy your heart with spiritual thoughts. For example, you may properly say to yourself, "I have gotten a whole day closer to death. What if it is the Lord God's will to call me during the coming night before His righteous Judgment Seat? Would I pass the test? In the morning I intended to pass the whole present day in a holy way, but did I? Have I somehow angered the Lord God?

After questioning yourself like this,

a) pray in your heart to the All-Holy Spirit that he may enlighten your mind and help you to remember accurately and in detail how you passed the day now coming to a close. That is, how you got up in the morning, how you got dressed, how you said your morning prayers, how you conducted yourself at work in the morning, how you conducted yourself during lunch, during rest after lunch, and in your treatment of your family, neighbors, and strangers. Especially, how did you conduct yourself with any person who is perilous for you, or in any circumstance that is perilous for you: did you expose yourself then to sin, or did your intentions to avoid sin weaken? How did you conduct yourself when you were treated rudely, were not obeyed, were laughed at, and in other such circumstances?

b) pray that the Holy Spirit may help you to remember accurately what you thought during the present day, what you said, what you did, how you tried or did not try to keep the holy resolution that you made in the morning to shun sin. What especially tended to draw you into sin or even succeeded in drawing you into it? What method did you undertake against the enticements of sin, or against the obstacles to fulfilling the will of God, and why did that method turn out to be inadequate?

c) pray that the Holy Spirit may help you to remember accurately how and why you sinned, what you failed to accomplish and why; whether you sinned by harboring foolish thoughts and desires in yourself; whether you sinned in words and deed; whether you sinned by neglecting to do something good or necessary; whether you sinned against the first commandment, against the second, against the third, and the rest; whether you took part in anyone else's sins, and so on.

Finally, d) pray especially that the Holy Spirit may help you to remember what special holy resolution you made in the morning and what helped you to fulfill it, or else what hindered or prevented you from fulfilling it and whether you took measures against the hindrances: what measures exactly, and why they turned out to be ineffective.

Our spiritual improvement depends precisely on such a diligent investigation of ourself. Without such a more or less scrupulous investigation of ourselves we cannot have spiritual improvement and no one should ever dream that without it he will perfect himself.

Thus calling to mind how you acted in the past day, adhere strictly to these guidelines: everything good that you find in yourself, consider not yours but God's, *for every good gift and every perfect gift is from above* (James 1:17), and from all your soul thank *the Father of lights* for this. Every foolish thing that you find in yourself ascribe to yourself, your weakness, and your foolish habits. Quickly repent of it, ask pardon of the Lord God, and again make a strong resolution not to sin, especially by the sin that you commit most frequently and eagerly, not to forget the Lord God, and to act circumspectly always and everywhere. Especially make the resolution to keep faithful watch over the chief bad proclivity of your heart, the one that you most often detect in yourself and that you find most pleasant. Then devise the most effective methods for avoiding whatever sins you committed and use these methods conscientiously. In particular, try to devise methods against your chief sin, the one to which you are disposed most of all.

At the same time, pray to the Lord God that He may think it fitting to reveal to you the most reliable methods through which, by His grace, you may be so strongly confirmed in your resolve and in unswerving fulfillment of the methods that you have devised that you would prefer to die rather than to commit your former sins again and to offend the Lord God again.

HOW SHOULD WE CONDUCT
ʹOURSELVES BEFORE SLEEP?

When you begin to feel that sleep is near, turn to the Lord God with your evening prayers, either using the prayers assigned by the holy Church or in your own words, different from those of the assigned prayers. But make sure that your prayers are without fail holy and thorough.

a) First of all thank the Lord God for every blessing that He has afforded you and everyone, for the Incarnation of the Lord Jesus Christ, for His sufferings and death, for our being given the holy Faith, for the holy Mysteries, and for all His internal and external, natural and supernatural guidance.

b) Pray that the Lord God may forgive you all your sins committed both this day and in past days as you forgive all those that have sinned against you. Pray especially fervently that he not allow you to die in your sins.

c) Pray that it may be His pleasure not to allow into your habitation our chief enemy with his malicious snares--dreams that are harmful to the soul and body--but may send you your guardian angel, who always prays for you, teaches you, and protects your soul and body from every evil.

d) Pray that the Lord may bless all those close to your heart: your parents, your brothers and sisters, all your family, your relatives, acquaintances, benefactors, friends, and enemies, and that he may bless all your spiritual and secular superiors.

e) Pray that the Lord may help the poor, those cast down in grief, travelers, the ill, and the aggrieved, that He may comfort the unfortunate, give shelter to orphans, strengthen the dying with hope, and give rest to the dead, that He may bless all children, guide all young people towards good deeds, strengthen in holy life all those of a mature age, and make all the elderly a model of holy life, that He may lead all sinners to repentance, extirpate the darkness in which the heathen, unbelievers, heretics, and schismatics live, that He may enlighten them with His light, bring them all to a knowledge of His truth, guide them all onto the true path of salvation, and save them.

Finally, put yourself entirely into the Lord God's hands, as you would if the present evening were the last in your life and if on rising in the morning you would have to stand before the judgment seat of God. Then make the sign of the cross on yourself and get into bed.

Never have a bed that is too soft. It is not a soft bed that gives sound sleep, but a clear conscience. Many sleep very badly on even the softest of feather-erbeds, while, on the other hand, others sleep very deeply and peacefully on very hard beds. A great many of the ancient Christian ascetics loved to sleep on the bare ground and to place a stone under their heads instead of a pillow. This is because a soft bed often serves as the faithful accomplice of the evil one in his actions against the purity of our souls and bodies. Why should we draw the evil one to ourselves, when he is so injurious to us, and when we should be constantly trying to repel him?

Try in every way possible to fall asleep thinking good thoughts. This is very important for the soul, as a familiar experience can attest: what you pour into the mill in the evening is what it grinds all night. All who look after themselves know very well that our last thoughts in the evening are usually the chief ones that stay with us during sleep and are the first ones we have in the morning. It is these thoughts mainly that are the cause of night-time fantasies; and it is by night-time fantasies that the evil one corrupts and destroys a great many. The evil one overlooks no opportunity for our destruction.

Most of all try to fall asleep in a spirit of devotion to the Lord God. If you fall asleep thus, then no matter what may happen to you during sleep, you have nothing to fear. Then you will sleep in the hands of God, as they say. The Lord God Himself will look after you and guard you, and no matter what misfortune might befall your body, your soul is safe--it is with the Lord God.

HOW SHOULD WE CONDUCT OURSELVES DURING SLEEPLESSNESS AT NIGHT?

If you cannot fall asleep for a long time after you go to bed, then, after lying down, try to imagine the Lord Jesus Christ in His sufferings on the cross and pray to Him in your heart about everything that comes into your heart: pray that the Lord God may deliver you and your family from all sins, from every evil will and from every sinful impurity, from deadly plague, from hunger, from lightning and storms, from sudden death, and especially from eternal death.

Pray that the Lord God may bring all sinners to heartfelt repentance and correction, that He may give to His Church faithful pastors who will zealously care for its purity, firmness, and glory, that He may subdue the enemies of His Church and persuade everyone of its purity and holiness, and that He may dispose everyone to sincere acceptance of its truth and principles.

Or try to imagine yourself at your death and think something like this: "If I were to die right now, what would become of me, who have sinned so greatly?" Or: "If I had to stand before the judgment seat of God in this present night, what could I expect, I who am so unworthy in God's eyes? Now I lie in bed and find it annoying that I have not been able to fall asleep for a long while; but how hard it will be to lie in hell if I go there because of my sins. In hell there is never any sleep, not even for a moment. There are very many entrances to hell, but there is not a single exit!" Occupy your mind with these and similar reflections until you fall asleep.

When you happen to wake up in the night, always turn your thoughts immediately to the Lord God, taking care lest foolish thought enter your heart; sign yourself with the sign of the cross and say, for example: "In the Name of the Father, and of the Son, and of the Holy Spirit. Amen. Lord Jesus Christ, Son of God, have mercy on me, a sinner! Lord Jesus Christ, for the sake of the prayers of Thy Most Pure Mother and of all Thy saints, have mercy on me. Amen."

If after this you do not fall asleep immediately, try hard to dismiss foolish thoughts from your mind, because there is no time in which our imagination likes to indulge in indecency more than when we cannot sleep at night. Try as quickly as possible to pray again about everything that may come into your mind.

And if, even after having done this, you do not fall asleep for a long time, it is better to get out of bed, stand before the holy icons and, if you can read, read psalms with attention and, when what is being read requires bows, make full prostrations. Or do full prostrations with the Jesus Prayer until you become fatigued or until peace enters your soul and you can again go to bed.

THE MOST IMPORTANT THING CONCERNING PRAYER

We often speak of prayer and, because it is one of the chief means of salvation, we should speak about it at length. But here we shall say only what is most necessary for our present purpose.

My friend, to pray in a God-pleasing way, always do these things:

1. When you pray, always imagine that the Lord God is standing invisibly right in front of you and is watching you. *For He*, as the holy apostle says, *is not*

far from every one of us; therefore, in Him we live, and move, and have our being (Acts 17:27,28).

2. Always pray only for what is pleasing to the Lord God or what is in agreement with God's will, for the Lord God answers only these prayers. The holy Apostle John says, *if we ask any thing according to his will, he heareth us* (I John 5:14). The holy Apostle James adds, *Ye ask, and receive not, because ye ask amiss, that ye may consume it upon your lusts* (James 4:3).

3. In prayer, freely tell the Lord God all your needs, with perfect humility and reverence, with firm hope of being heard, with complete love, with warm sincerity, and, if our prayer is not answered quickly, with grateful patience.

Pray with perfect humility and reverence because we are dependent on the Lord God for everything and because *He will regard the prayer of the destitute, and not despise their prayer* (Ps. 102:17 in KJV, 101:18 in LXX), *but He giveth grace unto the lowly* (Prov. 3:34).

Pray with a firm hope that you will be heard because the Lord God, being All-Good, readily gives a full hearing to everything that His children tell Him and because the holy Apostle says, *he that wavereth is like a wave of the sea driven with the wind and tossed. For let not that man think that he shall receive any thing of the Lord* (James 1:6, 7).

Pray with complete love because there is no one more worthy of our love than the Lord God.

Pray with warm sincerity because God is an omnipresent and omniscient Spirit, *Who therefore seeketh . . . worshippers . . . in spirit and in truth* (John 4:23) and because all who pray truly to Him always pray with their whole heart. The holy King David prayed to the Lord God like this: *I have cried with my whole heart; hear me, O Lord* (Ps. 118 [119]:145).

Pray with grateful patience because we are usually not very far-seeing and little know ourselves, while the Lord God knows well all the circumstances surrounding us and lying ahead of us, and He knows us incomparably better than we know ourselves. Therefore, He does not always immediately answer our prayers. Sometimes he does not answer them at all, but instead, in His wisdom and goodness, grants us something that we did not ask for, but which in our situation is more beneficial for the salvation of our souls.

The prayer that is most pleasing to the Lord God and most salvific for us is without a doubt the prayer that the Lord Himself taught us, that is, Our Father, Who art in the heavens, and so on.

Our Father. Father of everyone, including me.

May Thy name be recognized everywhere, and may it be glorified by the holiness of our hearts and lives.

May Thy kingdom and the kingdom of truth, righteousness, and blessedness be introduced everywhere, be strengthened, and dominate.

May Thy will be done in all the earth by all people, always as faithfully and zealously as it is done in heaven by Thy holy angels.

May Thy bread feed, strengthen, and preserve our lives, both corporal and spiritual.

May Thy mercy forgive us all our debts that we have amassed to this day in our recalcitrance and foolishness, and may it teach us to forgive each other debts of every kind.

May Thy goodness and Thine almightiness preserve us from every sin and from every occasion of sin and temptation, that we all may be made worthy to be in Thine eternal and all-blessed kingdom. Amen.

Pray this way with all your heart, and be completely assured that your prayer will be heard and answered. There are people (who are unworthy, however, of the name) who, not being able to understand how the Lord God can hear and answer our prayers, do not fully believe that He does hear and answer them. Do not pay attention to them. We do not understand how we live, but we certainly do live. Whoever in his error feels that he can help himself, let him do so. We, however, feel that we are weak and therefore should always turn in prayer to the All-powerful One, Who, in His always truthful word, tells us firmly, *Ask, and it shall be given you* (Matt. 7:7).

CONCLUSION

Dear friend, that is how you lead life in a God-pleasing, or holy, way. Here I have shown you how to pass only one day in a holy way. To show you how to pass another day in a holy way is unnecessary, because all earthly life, except Sundays and holy days, should be lived like this. Every thoughtful person should pass every day, in all seasons and at every stage of life, just this way. Because the evil one never stops trying to hurt us in any season or at any stage of life, and we therefore can never consider ourselves so free from sin and temptation for us not to fear becoming entangled in his snares, and falling or perishing.

HOW SHOULD WE SPEND SUNDAYS?

Sundays should be spent differently from other days of the week. Because all of us constantly benefit from God's many and various blessings, and constantly feel the need for new blessings, all of us are obliged by the word of God and the demand of our own consciences to raise our minds and hearts to the Lord God in the deepest reverence toward Him, in complete devotion to Him, and in the most profound gratitude and prayer. The holy King David said: *mine eyes are ever toward the Lord* (Ps. 24:15); *his praise shall continually be in my mouth* (Ps. 33:2); *and the meditation of my heart shall be before Thee for ever* (LXX) (Ps. 18:15). And the holy Apostle Paul commands us: *Pray without ceasing. In every thing give thanks. . . .* (I Thess. 5:17-18), and *always abounding in the work of the Lord* (I Cor. 15:58).

But just as the greater part of the human race still stands far below this perfection, the Lord God Himself, in order to raise it up little by little to this perfection, willed to set aside one day out of each week so that all of us would dedicate this day exclusively to the Lord God, putting aside on that day all activities that are more or less necessary to maintain our earthly life. In the Old Testament, this day was Saturday, and in the New, Sunday.

Saturday, the Sabbath day, was a day that was very sacred and strictly observed in the Old Testament. From Mount Sinai, amidst lightning, a thick cloud, and the deafening sound of a trumpet, the Lord God said to the whole throng of the sons of Israel, *Remember the sabbath day, to keep it holy. Six days shalt thou labour, and do all thy work: But the seventh day is the sabbath of the Lord thy God: in it thou shalt not do any work* (Exod. 20:8-10). *For whosoever doeth any work therein, that soul shall be cut off from among his people* (Exod. 31:14). *Six days may work be done; but in the seventh is the sabbath of rest, holy to the Lord: whosoever doeth any work in the sabbath day, he shall surely be put to death* (Exod. 31:15).

This commandment is quite clear and most fearsome, as shown by this incident: *And while the children of Israel were in the wilderness, they found a man that gathered sticks upon the sabbath day. And they . . . brought him unto Moses and Aaron . . . And the Lord said unto Moses, The man shall be surely put to death: all the congregation shall stone him with stones . . . and [they] stoned him with stones* (Num. 15:32-36).

The reason for the establishment of the Sabbath is shown in the Word of God to be a twofold one.

The first is contained in these words: *For in six days the Lord made heaven and earth, the sea, and all that in them is, and rested the seventh day: wherefore the Lord blessed the sabbath day, and hallowed it* (Exod. 20:11). That is, the Sabbath day was hallowed by God in memory of the creation of the world immediately after its creation, as related in the book of Genesis: *And on the sixth day God ended his work which he had made; and he rested on the seventh day from all his work which he had made. And God blessed the seventh day, and sanctified it: because that in it he had rested from all his work which God created and made* (Gen. 2:2-3). Since at the creation of the world there were still no nations, and the entire human race consisted of the father of the human race, Adam, anyone can understand that the Sabbath day was consecrated by the Lord God not for the Israelite people alone, and not for the Old Testament time alone, but for the entire human race and for all times. And therefore, this commandment obliges all people, even in the New Testament, to

114

its strictest fulfillment, wherever and whenever they might live, and obliges them just as strictly and absolutely as any other commandment of the Decalogue, of which it is the *fourth* commandment.

The other reason for the establishment of the Sabbath was the remembrance of the liberation of the people of Israel from Egyptian bondage: *Keep the sabbath day to sanctify it, as the Lord thy God hath commanded thee. Six days thou shalt labour, and do all thy work: But the seventh day is the sabbath of the Lord thy God: in it thou shalt not do any work, thou, nor thy son, nor thy daughter, nor thy manservant, nor thy maidservant . . . And remember that thou wast a servant in the land of Egypt, and that the Lord thy God brought thee out thence through a mighty hand and by a stretched out arm: therefore the Lord thy God commanded thee to keep the sabbath day* (Deut. 5:12-15). This commandment obliged the children of Israel alone to the observance of the Sabbath. But in the deliverance of the children of Israel from Egyptian bondage the holy apostles saw the deliverance of the human race from bondage to sin and death by the death of Jesus Christ (Gal. 4:31; 5:1), and therefore they also prescribed for us to consecrate or celebrate instead of the day of the Old Testament Sabbath the day of Resurrection—Sunday, which immediately follows it, because the death of the Lord ended and our deliverance began with His resurrection on the day immediately following the Sabbath day. And so, this day was called, and still is called, the day of Resurrection (in Russian,

Voskreseniye) and, in Church Slavonic, *Nedelya*, that is, the day on which we should not engage in activities necessary to maintain our earthly, physical life.

Both of these commandments are quite clear and most fearsome. The Lord God granted us six days out of every week to carry out business necessary for our earthly life, but the seventh day—only one day—He appointed for *rest* under pain of eternal death for violating it—appointed it, however, not for rest in general, but for *holy* rest, rest for the Lord God, that is, for rest that must be used for the Lord God, or for the glory of the Lord God.

Now, it is in itself obvious how we should spend, or rather dedicate or celebrate, Sunday. St. John Chrysostom says, "It was the Lord's good will to prescribe that we dedicate one day in the weekly cycle to spiritual matters." And in the book of the Acts of the Apostles we see that the original members of Christ's Church gathered on Sundays for the breaking of bread, and listened to Christ's teachings (Acts 20:7).

Thus, the *first* obligation that Sunday imposes on each of us is to set aside all the business that we need to engage in during the six days of the week to support our earthly lives. Fulfillment of this obligation is made the easier because the Lord God gave us six days out of every week to obtain what is necessary to maintain our earthly, physical lives. Besides, all works of charity, even though they might only effect maintenance of our earthy lives, are not prohibited even on

116

the seventh day, Sunday, and are even ordained as an obligation, as we see from the example and teaching of our Lord Jesus Christ Himself (Matt. 12:11, 12).

The *second* obligation, which Sunday imposes even more strictly on all of us, is to turn away from all impious acts that drive from our souls remembrance of the Lord God, reverence towards Him, devotion to Him, gratitude and a prayerful disposition of soul toward Him, to wit: all iniquitous works, and also all unedifying reading, all unedifying conversations, unedifying idleness and various games during which our souls often not only lose remembrance of the Lord God, but forget even themselves, give themselves up to a spirit of impiety and are carried away by delights, of which the undoubted end after death is bitter weeping and wailing (Luke 6:25).

The *third* obligation that the day of Resurrection places on us is, as is apparent from the example of the first Christians, attendance at the Sunday divine services, especially the Divine Liturgy. For among us there is not a single person on whom the Lord God has not bestowed His blessings at every moment and who could live even one minute without His blessings. For all our divine services consist in nothing else but remembrance of God's various blessings and in the expression of our reverence before the Lord God, our devotion to the Lord God, our grateful feelings toward Him, and our fervent prayer that His blessings upon us will continue. Only people with the most hardened, spiritually frozen, and dead hearts can not deeply feel and zealously fulfill the obligation for us to attend the divine services, especially the Liturgy, on Sundays. May the Lord God deliver all of us from this vile condition of soul.

The most reliable way to assure that our reverence towards the Lord God, our devotion, our gratitude, and our prayers to Him may become more alive, more sincere, more continuous, and stronger is to examine the cause of the Lord God's establishing the Sabbath in the Old Testament and Sunday in the New Testament. We must examine God's creation, and in it God's almightiness, His wisdom, and His goodness, and even more, God's ineffable love, shown to the human race by the passion and death of Jesus Christ, whereby He freed the human race from sin and death. And this is the *fourth* obligation that the Day of Resurrection, Sunday, imposes on us.

Contemplation of God's Creation

You can contemplate God's creation in the following way. Turn your eyes toward the earth. What a multitude of miracles of God's omnipotence, wisdom, and goodness are there. Who can count the kinds of trees, grasses, flowers, grains, and fruits of different varieties and qualities? Can all human efforts, even joining together, produce even one sapling, one flower, one kernel of grain, that would, having been thrown on the earth, open, grow up, form an ear, and give a multitude of new kernels, as happens as a matter of course? Who can enumerate all the species of animals, beasts, birds, fish, and insects? And who gave all of them such varied and wondrous characteristics and such an ability, in conformity with their nature, to find food for themselves, stay alive, and multiply their kind?

Besides this, what an innumerable multitude of God's almightiness, wisdom, and goodness must be hidden within our earth? The most determined human efforts have until now only touched the crust of the earth and yet what a multitude of valuable things has been uncovered!

Imagine the boundless seas. Who put a bulwark to their furious inundations and said, "Rage only up to this shore and no farther"? Who lays out rivers and springs over all the earth and gives us water to drink, without which we cannot live? Who forms rain clouds, leads them to where we live, and waters our fields and our gardens and orchards?

Who suspended our earth among the other heavenly bodies in such a way that they do not touch it and do not harm it? And who bears it by His own strength so that it is not deflected one bit from its orbit?

How limitless is God's power! God commands, and a terrible storm, that had arisen in a minute, breaks age-old oaks like half-dried reeds and scatters our dwellings like wood-shavings. God commands, and such strong thunder sounds that the earth shakes and all of nature trembles. God commands, and the fruitful earth with all its growing plants is covered with snow or ice, so that not the slightest signs of life can be discerned on it. God commands, and this land, lifeless until now, is reborn and bears such a multitude of fruits that all the millions of living creatures: cattle, wild beasts, insects, birds, and human beings are nourished with its plenty for the whole year.

Turn your gaze to heaven. What an amazing spectacle we see there! Who can count the vast multitude of stars and measure their extraordinary size and distance from our earth? Even with our naked eyes we see more than we would be able to count. But when we equip our eyes with telescopes, they appear to us to be huge and really innumerable.

Finally, raise your mind up to the highest heaven, to the indescribable habitation of the powers on high and of our God Himself. What an innumerable multitude of pure Spirits fly around him there, and drink in from Him their life, light, strength, joy, and blessedness, and being filled with these, sing, *Blessing, and glory, and wisdom, and thanksgiving, and honour, and power, and might, be unto our God for ever and ever. Amen* (Rev. 7:12).

Such contemplation of God's creations says very poignantly, powerfully, and deeply to the very heart of each of us who is attentive, "Fall into the dust before the Creator of the universe and pray to Him, the Almighty, Most-Wise and All-Good, with the most profound reverence. When you look at heaven and earth, do not dare to look upon this most magnificent collection of the wondrous works of God without sincere emotion and prayer. And when you contemplate God's creation, do not stop up your ears, but rather listen attentively, as every blade of grass on earth and every star in the heavens tells you, along with the prophet, *What God is as great as our God?* (Ps. 76:14); *How good is God to Israel* (Ps. 72:1); *Of His understanding there is no measure* (Ps. 146: 5); Worship Him with your whole soul."

Such contemplation of God's creations says very poignantly, powerfully, and deeply to the very heart of each of us who is attentive, "Feel your mortality, your sinfulness, your nothingness, and learn humility. Who are you in comparison with the Almighty? How small is the circle of your activity! How limited is your power! But you sometimes dare to take pride in the power of your activity. How nearsighted and often senseless is your intellect! But you sometimes dare to pride yourself in your earthly wisdom and insight, as if you were no less intelligent than God! How insignificant you are among such a multitude of God's creations! But you sometimes dare to pride yourself in earthly greatness, the splendor of your home, the beauty of your clothing, and so on, as if you had rights no less than God's. You often think that people like you, who are often very stupid, but almost always more or less blind, insult you by not considering you smarter and better than they. Can it really be that other people cannot be smarter and better than you? My friend, this is boundless pride. Wisdom and insight are God's gifts, and God gives them to whom He wishes (I Cor. 12: 4,12). Might He not give them to whomever He may wish in a greater degree than he gave them to you? He divides His gifts *severally*, that is, completely at will (I Cor. 12:11). If you do not stop taking pride in yourself, you will lose the one distinction that alone might elevate you: you will lose your reason."

Such contemplation of God's creations says very poignantly, powerfully, and deeply to the very heart of each of us who is attentive, "In spite of all your insignificance, feel also your greatness and your dignity. He Who created heaven, this sun, these stars, this earth with all its fruits is your Father, Who loves you more tenderly than even the most tender mother could ever love her children, Who cares so greatly about your salvation that it seems He could not be happy without you, and Who has prepared for you the eternal, blessed kingdom with Himself. How can you not see your greatness! How can you not strive for the unimaginable blessedness prepared for you, but instead you use all your reason, all your strength, and all your time only to obtain earthly contentment—ashes and dust. Do not forget: you are of divine descent. You need to draw near to God continually and earnestly. God is the source of your happiness. Only in Him can you find perfect satisfaction for your heart, which continually thirsts for happiness. Do not think, say, or especially do anything that may distance you from the Almighty, Most Wise, and All-Good Creator, but try to have in your thoughts, to say and do, only what brings you closer to your Creator."

Such contemplation of God's creations further says very poignantly, powerfully, and deeply to the very heart of each of us who is attentive, "Try with all your might to do the will of the Almighty, Most Wise, and All-Good Creator. May fulfillment of His will be your most important and most beloved task. In nature, everything obeys the will of the Creator. Neither heaven nor earth deviates from His will by a single hair. Submit conscientiously to every one of His words with childlike obedience. Take care to become a participant in the kingdom of God, among the multitudes of His obedient and zealous servants. Any one of God's creations may become hostile and punish you. The earth may instantaneously open and swallow you, as it many times before has opened and swallowed those disobedient to God the Creator."

Finally, such contemplation of God's creations further speaks very poignantly, powerfully, and deeply to the very heart of each of us who is attentive, "You who love God: follow the path onto which the Lord has directed you and fear nothing. Is the whole world against you? Do not fear, but only try to please the Lord God, and then, remembering the words of the holy Apostle, *If God be for us, who can be against us?* (Rom. 8:31), remain completely calm. Does the evil one with all the wrath of hell rise up against you? Do not be afraid, just try to avoid all occasions of sin, through which our enemy always more easily lures us into his nets and ruins us. And then, when you need to struggle with your enemy, struggle with him with all your might, sparing nothing, and if, during your struggle, you feel a lack of sharpness of mind, of courage of spirit, or of the strength of your body, immediately pray to the Lord God and be quite sure that you will receive everything that you need. Because God, *that spared not His own Son, but delivered Him up for us all, how shall He not with Him also freely give us all things?* says the holy Apostle (Rom. 8:32). Do not be afraid.

Contemplation of the Passion and Death of Our Lord

You may contemplate the passion and death of the Lord in this way. The last sufferings of the Lord began with sorrow in His soul. Having gone up with His disciples onto the Mount of Olives, He said: *My soul is exceeding sorrowful, even unto death* (Matt. 26:38).

Christ then saw clearly that He was going to unspeakable tortures and to the most deplorable death. He saw clearly then that the Jewish people, which had always been loved by Him, which had been chosen by Him and had enjoyed His greatest benevolence, but which now had become the perpetrator of His agonizing death, would be subjected to a terrible judgment. He saw clearly that, in spite of all their importance, His passion and death would be in vain for many millions of people blinded by paganism and by the darkness of other such false teachings. He saw clearly that His passion and death for very many people within Christianity itself, who had lost their

124

minds from various passions and had therefore fallen into the most coarse excess and impious life, would serve not for salvation, which He very much desired, but only for greater condemnation. The sorrow in Christ's soul was now very heavy and agonizing.

In such deep sorrow, withdrawing a little from His disciples, and throwing Himself on the ground, He prayed, *O My Father, if it be possible, let this cup pass from Me: nevertheless not as I will, but as Thou wilt* (Matt. 26:39). This prayer of Christ was so profound and ardent that during it sweat fell from His body to the ground like drops of blood (Luke 22:44). He ceased this prayer only when He saw clearly that His Father did not see fit to free Him from the cup of suffering prepared for Him and that the betrayer and the soldiers had already drawn near to take Him to torments and death.

Pilate would have liked to have freed Christ from any punishment because he clearly saw His innocence. But as he, in the weakness and duplicity of his pagan character, could not do this, he turned Christ over to the soldiers to be beaten, with the intention of mollifying, by the wounds given Him, the Jews, who were embittered against Him (John 19:1). The soldiers took Christ from the hall of judgment to the Praetorium and, of course, to the satisfaction of the Jews, gathered their whole detachment for His beating (Mark 15:16). The beating took place, without a doubt, in the way that it was done among the Romans, that is, having stripped Christ's clothing to the hips, the soldiers tied Him to a pillar and beat Him with all their might with whips, which were usually made of leather thongs in order to tear the body being beaten as quickly and deeply as possible. To please the Jews even more, the Roman soldiers were not satisfied with only beating the innocent Christ; after His condemnation by Pilate to crucifixion, they thought up a new kind of torment: *and when they had plaited a crown of thorns, they put it upon His head* (Matt. 27:29), *and they smote Him on the head with a reed* (Mark 15:19). It is quite painful when you only slightly prick your hand or foot with a thorn. But the the Savior's pain was incomparable. When the crown of thorns was placed on the Savior's head, its thorns pierced His head from all directions; then they beat His head, covered with the crown of thorns, with a stick. It was an exceedingly severe pain.

In addition, Christ also felt similar pain because He had been handed over to these torments by one of His disciples, been rejected by another of them, while all the rest had fled in fear; because the pursuers had bound Him and led Him bound from one judge to the other; because in His very presence the Jews had sought out false witnesses to accuse Him and subjected Him to the most malicious mockery; because the soldiers had clothed Him in purple like a King, had put a reed in His hand, and had knelt before Him and cried, *Hail, King of the Jews!* (Matt. 27:29); because He had then been slapped and spit in the face, and that out of disdain for Him, the notorious robber Barabbas had been preferred over Him; because He had been condemned to crucifixion and been crucified between two robbers, as if He were their leader and chief; and finally, because the high priests and scribes so raged against Him that nothing could mollify them, and because they, in the face of all Pilate's attempts to protect Him, only sank into greater madness and bitterness and cried wildly, *crucify Him, crucify Him* (John 19:6).

After these torments they led Christ outside of the city to the place of execution, to Golgotha. On His shoulders the soldiers put the cross, consisting of at least two rather long and, of course, heavy beams of wood. But under this burden, after a cruel flogging, and accompanied on all sides by the curses and malicious mockery of the Jews, Christ had to have soon become exhausted, and He did. A stranger who was encountered along the way, Simon of Cyrene, was forced to carry His cross (Matt. 27:32). Christ Himself, already half-dead, came to the place of execution. Here the soldiers again removed His clothing and nailed His hands and feet to the cross. He hung on the nails, which from the weight of His body constantly enlarged the wounds and increased the pain in His hands and feet. What terrible torment! The crown of thorns on His head, the wounds from the nails in His hands and feet, the wounds from the whips on His back and sides, and dislocations in many of His members all caused severe pain. He was covered with blood, which poured onto the ground.

Three hours passed in this condition. How indescribably hard those three hours were. Finally, He said, *It is finished*, bowed his head, and gave up His spirit (John 19:30, Matt. 27:50). In examining these sufferings of the Lord, none of us can escape the most profound agitation of heart. For these sufferings say to each of us, "Behold *how God so loved the world, that He gave His only begotten Son, that whosoever believeth in Him should not perish, but have everlasting life* (John 3:16). Can there be a love greater than this love? And should not this love awaken in us love in response?"

Nothing so strongly draws our hearts to love as does love. And Our Lord's love for us is a love that cannot be compared with any other love and is truly inexpressible and divine.

Upon seeing these sufferings of the Lord, our hearts, if they have not yet become completely coarse, are very deeply pierced with a feeling of gratitude to Him, love for and devotion to Him, reverence before Him, and submission to Him. For He says to each of us by His sufferings, "I suffered not for Myself, but for you and for all people, so that you and all people, in gratitude, love, and devotion to Me, would turn away from sin, and in order to turn away from sin would also bear deprivation, labors, and sorrows of every kind and never give entrance into your heart to sin. I know that the world does not love those who are devoted to Me and together with the chief enemy of your salvation tries to draw you away from Me, especially by the various troubles, deprivations, labors, and sorrows of life. Do not mind these, but have courage, stand firmly, in no case lose patience or hope, and constantly look to Me! Every time that some misfortunes attack you and you are forced to drink a couple drops of misery, remember that I, the Only-Begotten Son of God, and your God, had to drink the whole cup of the most revolting bitterness. You see yourself abandoned by everyone and you have no comfort? This happened to Me, too: even My most beloved disciples abandoned Me. I was abandoned even by God, My Father. Your heart is greatly oppressed by some misfortune that has beset you or threatens you? It is not worse than what My heart felt on the Mount of Olives. Do enemies offend you, slander you, curse and revile you? It was the same with Me. Your good deeds are not remembered and are repaid not only with ingratitude, but even with evil deeds? The Jews repaid Me for My good deeds in the same way. You are not respected and the unworthy are preferred over you? It was the same with Me. Even the inveterate robber Barabbas was preferred over Me. People do not believe in your innocence, in spite of your justifications? They did not believe Me either. Are you forced to live with coarse and hostile people? They are no more coarse or hostile than those I lived with. Are you exhausted under the weight of your sufferings? I also was exhausted under the weight of My Cross. Do you struggle with shortages and poverty? I also barely had only the most necessary things, and finally was deprived even of them, deprived even of My last piece of clothing. Are you downcast that your clothing is not as good as others have? Look at Me. I am covered only with wounds and blood, My adornment only nails and a crown of thorns. Are you ill and poorly taken care of? Are you constantly worrying, and spend nights without sleep? I also often did not sleep, and My last night I spent completely without sleep, and at that time I also suffered beatings and heard curses and ridicule; when I suffered burning thirst, My drink was gall and vinegar; My bed was only nails and the cross. In a word, during all your troubles look at Me. I suffered and endured everything, and soon all My sufferings were replaced by blessedness and glory. Look at Me. In looking at Me, you will find such strength against your sufferings that you will suffer not only with patience, but with love, because My words will constantly be in your immediate memory: *ye shall be sorrowful, but your sorrow shall be turned into joy. . . your heart shall rejoice, and your joy no man taketh from you* (John 16:20, 22). *Where I am, there shall also My servant be*" (John 12:26).

The first members of Christ's Church, as the book of the Acts of the Apostles shows, spent Sunday listening to the Word of God (Acts 20:7). Hearing or reading the Word of God is necessary for all of us and is the *fifth* obligation imposed on each of us by the day of Resurrection. For all of us without exception are obliged to live a holy life. *[God] hath chosen us in Him before the foundation of the world, that we should be holy and without blame before Him,* says the holy Apostle Paul (Eph. 1:4). But none of us can live a holy life unless we hear or read the Word of God, for only in the Word of God are shown the rules of holy life.

Many, many people who lived in the world senselessly and died without repentance would have tried zealously to live in a holy way and would not have found themselves in the torments of hell if during their lives they had practiced reading or hearing the Word of God.

Upon an attentive and zealous reading or hearing of the Word of God, each of us can quickly receive light from God with which to comprehend more soundly the Word of God and quickly see the image of a holy life in it as in a mirror, and see the vices in ourselves, especially our chief passion, which hinders us most of all from behaving blamelessly and in a holy way. By this reading or hearing, anyone may also quickly see clearly the means for extracting his soul from its dangerous state and also receive from the Lord God a firm desire and the strength to firmly adhere to a holy life.

We should not forget, however, that some people, in reading the word of God, have fallen into various errors and have perished. Others have read the the word of God frequently, but it did not produce a saving effect on their hearts, and they also perished. To avoid such misfortune, observe these guidelines as you settle down to read or hear the Word of God with the proper reflection:

1) First of all, pray to the Lord God that He will enlighten your mind and heart with His light. Pray as is proper, that is, with absolute reverence, with faith, with your whole heart, and constantly imagining that He were standing right in front of you.

2) Then, get the interpretation of St. John Chrysostom or another holy father for the passage that you desire to read. Read the passage, or ask someone else to read it if you yourself cannot read, and stop at the first truth that you do not quite understand.

3) Having read or having read the truth, linger on it and look into your heart: do you believe the truth that you read or heard? If you find that you believe, give thanks to the Lord God for this grace and at the same time pray to Him that He will also preserve you in this faith. If you find that your faith is weak, pray again immediately to the Lord with all your soul that He may grant you faith in the truth that you read or heard and strengthen faith in you. *Faith. . . is the gift of God* (Eph. 2:8); and *every perfect gift is from above*, as another holy apostle affirms, *and cometh down from the Father* in answer to our prayer to Him (James 1:17).

4) Strengthen your faith in the truth that you have read or heard, look to see what this truth contains, whether it is simply a teaching or if it is a Divine commandment.

5) If the truth that has been read consists simply of a teaching, ask yourself, "What does the text say here? Did I think of it this way before? Doesn't this truth give me some instruction?"

For example, let us say that we have read the following words from the Holy Gospel: *After this manner therefore pray ye: Our Father Who art in heaven.* Ask yourself, "What does the text say here?" It says that God is a Father. Then begin to contemplate, for example, thus: "If God is a Father, then His heart must be a father's heart, tender, filled with love, mercy, and paternal feelings." "Here it also says that He is not my, your, or his Father, but ours; consequently, He is the Father of every human being, whoever, wherever, from wherever, and whatever he may be. Have I thought of it this way before? Hardly ever. Because, although I have indeed heard that God is a Father and have even called Him Father in prayer, I called Him that almost without sense, that is, I called God Father, not understanding what I was saying. Do not these words give me some instruction? Yes, they give very important instruction. About what? About this: if God is the Father of every human, then there is no doubt that every man, whoever he may be, is my brother, and every woman or girl is my sister; consequently I behaved very foolishly if I treated some people as strangers, and did not find them deserving of even a glance or word, or considered them the kind of people to whom I do not owe any love. I acted very foolishly, and I must correct myself, otherwise I must not dare to pray using this Lord's Prayer, and therefore, must not consider myself as belonging to the number of true children of the Father God. And what will become of me if I do not correct myself?!"

6) If the truth that you have read contains some kind of Divine command or commandment then say to yourself, "What am I being told here? Why must I behave this way? When must I behave this way? What will happen to me if I do not begin behaving this way?"

For example, you read or hear, *Judge not, that ye be not judged* (Matt. 7:1). Ask yourself, "What is this passage saying?" It says that it is forbidden to judge. "Whom?" Anyone. "That is not obvious." Of course it is obvious. In this passage judgment is forbidden altogether, and no exception is made for anyone; consequently, in this passage it is forbidden to judge anyone.

"But what if another person lives and behaves badly, giving temptation?" Do not judge! No one is permitted to judge.

"But the temptation may cause great harm to morality."

Of course it may, but do not judge; find a suitable time and try in a brotherly way to admonish the tempter. A brotherly admonition is not forbidden. But if he does not listen to you, think who has the right to admonish him more strongly. Tell his superior. Superiors have the right not only to admonish, but also to pass judgment. Let his superiors admonish or judge and punish him. You, on the other hand, should abide in peace and take care that you not behave as the tempter does. "Why may I not judge?" The passage, *that ye be not judged* tells us why. "What is the reason for this?" We are not told this, but of course there is a reason. "What is the reason?" This, for example, is a reason: whoever loves to look at others and keep an eye on what they are doing almost as a rule forgets himself, and in forgetting himself, usually does not see his own faults. And not seeing his own faults, he always deems himself better than others. But whoever has fallen into such a state judges and condemns everyone, sparing no one, and often condemns his own superiors, who are given the right of judgment, and he sometimes condemns even the Judge of all, God. "How can it be so?" It is so, because the state in which such a person who condemns finds himself is pride, and pride is the mother of sins. *Pride is the beginning of sin, and he that hath it shall pour out abomination*, says the Wise One (Ecclus. 10:13). "So, I have very often and seriously sinned by judgment. I must correct myself and by no means condemn others; otherwise the Lord will constantly condemn me, and He will say the words, *Depart from Me, ye cursed, into everlasting fire* (Matt. 25:41), to me and all the other goats like me."

7. After this, in order that you may be completely assured of the correctness of your contemplation, read an interpretation by a holy father of the Church of the passage of the Word of God that you were contemplating. Then think over the words that the holy father says in the same way you did the scriptural passage.

8. After this contemplation, always form in yourself repentance for the sin that you examined and make a firm intention to change. But do not allow

this firm intention to remain only in your mind, but try to carry it out in reality; as soon as you find that you are not carrying it out or have forgotten it, renew it again in your memory and put forth a new effort to carry it out.

9. If you cannot contemplate a truth that stands out from all the others in your reading, then with a clear conscience you can read or listen further and take another truth or even some other edifying book for contemplation.

Note. When you begin to read an edifying book, read it in order from beginning to end, and never read as some do, reading only here and there. Because sober-minded writers often place some very useful truths in the beginning of a book, without which what is written in the middle or towards the end often cannot be understood with the appropriate clarity and definiteness.

10. When you begin reflection, do not be doubtful or too distrustful of yourself, thinking that you cannot reflect, because you can quickly teach yourself to reflect, and once you have learned, it will become easy and pleasant for you.

11. Every reflection must always end with prayer, because the holy Apostle commands us, *In every thing give thanks* (IThess. 5:18). And how can we not give thanks for the saving Divine light that we have received.

As we must examine ourselves every day in relation to our salvation, so much the more should it be our obligation on Sundays. And this is the *sixth* obligation that Sunday imposes on each of us. Sunday before all other days should be a day on which we make the most attentive and detailed examination of our spiritual state in relation to salvation, and make a new, firm intention to root out from ourselves everything opposed to God and our salvation.

AFTERWORD

In fervently trying to form yourself in a holy and blameless life, you must constantly remember that the holiness and blamelessness of our lives must be the fruit of our wholehearted love for the Lord God. For the holy apostle said that God the Father hath chosen us in him before the foundation of the world, that we should be holy and without blame before him in love (Eph. 1:4). Therefore we must first of all and most of all strive to acquire love for the Lord God. Everything relating to holiness and blamelessness of life is valid, sound, and efficacious only if we have love for the Lord God. Without love for the Lord God, everything is insufficient, weak, or even worthless (I Cor. 13:1-3). Therefore, love for the Lord God is the chief commandment. Whoever has acquired true love for the Lord God has acquired true holiness and true blamelessness of life, for love is the union of perfection.

Note: In the Old Testament, besides the Sabbath Day, certain other sacred days were also established for celebration, such as Passover, Pentecost, Purification, and others. It was commanded that all of these days be spent in the same way as were Sabbath days. Likewise in the New Testament not only Sundays but other days as well were established for celebration to the glory of God and in honor of the Mother of God and other saints. All of these feast days were established equally for the glory of God and for the salvation of our souls. Therefore, my friend, spend all these days in a manner just as holy and salvific as you spend every Sunday. Your soul is priceless: take care of it. Do not pay attention to people who in our time often do not honor the Lord's feasts. The Lord, it is true, does not punish them, but He does not punish people in the present life for other serious offenses as well. By not punishing them, the Lord shows not that He approves or does not find their behavior reprehensible, but shows His long-suffering, not willing that any should perish, but that all should come to repentance (II Pet. 3:9); or perhaps He has already abandoned them, and together with the angels which kept not their first estate, but left their own habitation, He has reserved them unto the judgment and eternal fire (Jude 6). *Fret not thyself because of evildoers. . . For evildoers shall be cut off* (Ps. 37:1, 9).

BIOGRAPHY OF METROPOLITAN GREGORY

etropolitan Gregory (in the world, Gregory Petrovich Postnikov) was born on 1 November 1784 in the village of Mikhaylovskoye in Nikitskiy district of Moscow province in the family of a deacon. He studied at Perervinskiy and Holy Trinity seminaries and received his higher education in the St. Petersburg Ecclesiastical Academy, from which he graduated in 1814. He embraced monasticism immediately after completing his course of study. Postnikov's tonsure was performed on 25 August 1814. He was ordained a hierodeacon on 2 September and a hieromonk on the 28th. Embracing monasticism was the heart's desire of the young man, who was inclined to reflection and asceticism.

In 1817, Fr. Gregory was assigned rector of the Monastery of St. Joseph of Volokolamsk with elevation to the rank of archimandrite. Even so, he did not abandon his scholarly work at the Academy.

The consecration of Archimandrite Gregory (Postnikov) as bishop of Revel and suffragan of the St. Petersburg diocese took place on 7 May 1822. By an ukase of the Holy Synod, the administration of the St. Sergius Hermitage near St. Petersburg also was placed in his care. In 1825, Vladyka Gregory was assigned to an independent see, ruling the Kaluga diocese until 1829. In 1827, Bishop Gregory began to combine his labors in administering the diocese with work in the Most Holy Synod.

Upon his elevation to the rank of archbishop, he was transferred to the diocese of Ryazan, which he headed from 1829 to 1831. Archbishop Gregory then labored in Tver' for 17 years (1831-1848) and exerted considerable effort in teaching the Tver' flock the Word of God. He devoted special attention to overcoming the Old Ritualist schism. Often and regularly visiting various, at times quite remote, corners of his diocese, Vladyka Gregory entered the schismatic sketes and prayer houses and held discussions with well known

Old Ritualist dogmatists, posing them questions concerning dogma, rituals, and church history. Working with persuasion and avoiding any coercive measures, the archpastor gained respect even among the hardened schismatics, and they sincerely regretted when the "great pope" was transferred from Tver' to Kazan. The Orthodox flock parted with their hierarch literally with tears. This is how Vladyka Gregory's biographer M. Shavrov described the event:

The leave-taking of the pastor from his flock took place on 25 March [1848] in the Tver cathedral after Vespers. On account of the flooding of the rivers, Tver' had been divided into several parts and between them there was no communication, but even inhabitants of parts distant from the cathedral wanted to accompany their archpastor, if only from afar and, if only from afar, to receive his blessing. The inhabitants of the parts across the Volga gathered on the banks of the Volga, near the church of St. Philip the Apostle, from whence there is a view to the cathedral; the inhabitants of the parts across the Tmaka, near the church of St. Nicholas the Wonderworker, from whence there is also a view of the cathedral; the inhabitants of the main part of the city gathered in the cathedral itself and filled the entire square adjacent to it. The Archbishop himself was touched to the depth of his soul at this occurrence, and owing to strong emotion could not finish his farewell speech to the flock. The farewell "many years" for the departing archpastor also could not be finished owing to the strong state of emotion of the protodeacon. When the Archbishop went out onto the cathedral porch in his mantiya with his staff in hand and blessed the people who had gathered on the square and on the banks of the flooded rivers, the Volga and the Tmaka, all the people fell prostrate as they received the blessing" (M. Shavrov, Preosvyashchennyy Grigoriy, mitropolit Novgorodskiy i Sankt-Peterburgskiy, St. Petersburg, 1860, pp. 9-10).

Such a touching farewell from the flock to its archpastor is explained not only by the fact that Vladyka Gregory had served for a rather long time in Tver' and the people had become attached to him. In leaving the diocese, he did indeed leave a good memory of himself. In general, having set out on the path of hierarchical service, Vladyka Gregory was forced to act in a way that overcame his natural disposition. By nature he was a person of a somewhat severe mold, an ascetic and a man of prayer. He loved solitude, which he often had to sacrifice, since the service of a bishop demanded from him frequent appearance among people. As a hierarch, he had to instruct both pastors and faithful, addressing them with a word of edification. And Vladyka often associated with God's people at services in church, accompanying the divine service with short, but remarkably clear and easily understood sermons. Vladyka Gregory did not limit himself to occasions when the clergy and the people came to him in the cathedral, but he himself also went out among the people, spending time in numerous journeys throughout the diocese.

He devoted special attention to selection of clergy. In his diocese, the practice of ordaining worthy clerics approached the order that once existed in the ancient church. Vladyka considered that the best pastors were those whom the community, the parish, had unanimously chosen from their midst. Thus, the archpastor followed the reaction of the flock to the choice of this or that candidate. In instances where some among the parishioners were unhappy with the candidate, the ordination was postponed or did not take place at all. Such an approach was a rarity at that time and even today is not frequently applied. But in any case Vladyka Gregory considered it possible to proclaim "Axios" during ordination to the diaconate or the priesthood only when the people from their whole hearts could answer him, "Axios! (Worthy!)," approving the ordination of their future pastor.

While ruling the Tver' diocese, Archbishop Gregory furthered the restoration of the ancient Orsh Monastery, which had fallen into decline. Archbishop Gregory of Tver' took a leading role in the cause of the glorification of the God-pleasing hierarch Mitrofan, bishop of Voronezh, which took place in 1832.

Vladyka Gregory's service in Kazan lasted from 1848 to 1856. This period of his life was signified by activity in converting the Tatar population to Orthodoxy and provision of spiritual literature to Orthodox Tatars in their native language. Under the oversight of Archbishop Gregory a special commission formed at the Kazan Ecclesiastical Academy carried out the translation of Sacred Scripture and liturgical books into the Tatar language.

In August 1856, in connection with the coronation of Emperor Alexander II, Archbishop Gregory was raised to the rank of metropolitan "for many years of archpastoral service, judicious zeal, and indefatigable activity in the word and example of piety, in the edification of pastors and flock, in the preparation of bearers of the good tidings of the faith of Christ, and in the enlightenment of straying children of the Church." In autumn of the same year, Vladyka Gregory was, in accordance with the will of the Sovereign, transferred to the cathedra of the capital. His title now became "Metropolitan of Novgorod, Saint Petersburg, Estonia, and Finland, Sacred Archimandrite of the Holy Trinity Alexander Nevskiy Lavra." From his first steps in his new post Metropolitan Gregory had to exert considerable effort to protect his flock, especially the part of it that belonged to higher society, from the influence of Catholic propaganda, which had intensified in Russia during the era of Alexander's reforms. While still in his capacity of bishop of Revel, Vladyka Gregory had had to struggle with Western influence on Russian society, when he, as president of a committee composed of the most educated representatives of the Orthodox clergy, undertook efforts to limit the growing popularity of various types of translated writings of a mystical character, far from Orthodox and often from Christian tradition, such as the works of

Boehme, Stilling, Eckhardtshausen and others. He spoke against the ideas and opinions popularized by the "Sionskiy Vestnik" and similar periodicals.

Metropolitan Gregory appeared before the St. Petersburg flock as a preacher of repentance. The call to repentance sounds in many of his sermons and homilies. Thoughts of the necessity of changing one's life runs as a theme through his writings. The arch-pastor, called to service in the capital in his declining years, none the less labored with youthful zeal for the Lord, unsparingly, for he saw that alongside the good changes in social life new, quite undesirable currents were penetrating in the consciousness of society and more widely, into the masses of the people,: a frivolous attitude towards life, the lowering of moral criteria, a forgetting of the ordinances of ancestral piety. The metropolitan of St. Petersburg often had to speak to his flock with a word of denunciation. His articles, printed in the journal "Spiritual Talks," were compiled under the expressive headings "Candles into the dark and gloom" and "Light into the dark and gloom."

In the words of a contemporary, Vladyka Gregory was a "moral martyr." He devoted all his strength to service to the Church with nothing left over, resting his soul only during the hours of the divine services.

Among incessant troubles and cares for the needs of his flock and his excessive labors, the arch-pastor approached the end of his earthly existence. In the beginning of June 1860, Vladyka caught a serious cold but in spite of his ailment continued for a time to do his usual work. It seemed that he would be able to come through his illness safely. But the Lord judged otherwise. The illness became worse, and in the night of 16-17 June 1860, after receiving the Holy Mysteries, Metropolitan Gregory reposed in the Lord.

In his funeral oration, one of Metropolitan Gregory's fellow laborers characterized the activity and personality of the reposed hierarch thus: "Service to God was the delight of your life, and zeal for the glory of His name consumed your soul. In days of joy and sorrow, in days of God's mercies and His dread visitations, you were present with prayer and the Bloodless Sacrifice before the altar of God. In the service of God your soul knew not weariness, and you, zealous to the end of your life, were zealous for God the Savior and for the increase of His Holy Church."

Metropolitan Gregory was buried in the Annunciation Church of the St. Alexander Nevskiy Lavra.

Vladyka Gregory was an eminent hierarch. In the course of his whole life, along with doing his archpastoral duties, he also wrote scholarly and homiletic works and occupied himself with religious education. Being professor of St. Petersburg Theological Academy, he composed notes on dogmatic theology, and wrote and defended a doctoral dissertation.

In the center of Vladyka Gregory's scholarly interests always was the theme of the defense of Orthodox dogma from attacks from schismatics and the heterodox. The chief work of his life, "The Truly Ancient and Truly Orthodox Church of Christ," which ran into several editions, bears a vividly expressed apologetic character. The learned hierarch was guided by the same desire to show the truth of the Orthodox Christian faith clearly and in a well-grounded way when he reported to the Most Holy Synod in 1859 of the necessity of compiling a scholarly work that would prove to any impartial reader the truth of Orthodoxy. He called all Russian theologians to the creation of such a work and donated significant capital from his personal funds, designated to encourage participants.

Soon after his move to the cathedra of Kazan, Vladyka Gregory accomplished the publication of sermons that he had written from 1826 to 1848. This collection comprised five volumes and was published under the title Sermons or Talks for all Sundays and Feast Days with the Addition of Sermons and Talks for Certain Special Occasions.

Besides compositions of an apologetic and homiletic character, Metropolitan Gregory compiled the lives of Sts. Guriy, Archbishop of Kazan, and Barsonofiy, Bishop of Tver rendering by this hagiographical work a worthy tribute of respect to his holy predecessors on the cathedras of Kazan and Tver.

Vladyka Gregory played an important role in the rise of Russian church periodicals. In 1821 the first religious magazine in Russia, "Khristianskoye chteniye (Christian Reading)," published at the St. Petersburg Theological Academy, was established by his efforts. In answer to his petition in 1855, permission was granted for the publication at the Kazan Theological Academy of the journal "Pravoslavniy sobesednik (Orthodox Interlocutor)."

In 1857, Metropolitan Gregory petitioned the Synod for permission for publication of a weekly journal, "Dukhovnaya beseda (Spiritual Discussion)," at the ecclesiastical seminary in St. Petersburg; it began publication in 1858. In this publication, a chronicle of events in church life and of government orders from the Department of the Orthodox Faith began to be published for the first time in Russia.

The portrait of Vladyka Gregory (Postnikov) would be incomplete if we did not mention that the venerable hierarch was distinguished by extreme unacquisitiveness. More than modest in his daily life, he gave abundant alms to the needy and spent his salary on works of charity. An event in his life is well known in which Emperor Nicholas I allotted a one-time allowance of two thousand rubles to the hierarch, who had found himself without means for subsistence.

From 1824 through 1856, Vladyka Gregory was an honorary member of the Council of the Imperial Philanthropic Society, and was its chief trustee and president from 1856 until his death.

The book "A Day of Holy Life, or the Answer to the Question, How Can I Live a Holy Life?" was first published in St. Petersburg in 1856. In 1904, it came out in a third edition, from which our book is printed.

A. Svetozarskiy